MAXIMIZE
YOUR
MEMORY

BY RAMÓN CAMPAYO

CAREER
PRESS

This edition first published in 2010 by Career Press, an imprint of
Red Wheel/Weiser, LLC
With offices at:
65 Parker Street, Suite 7
Newburyport, MA 01950
www.redwheelweiser.com
www.careerpress.com

ISBN: 978-1-60163-117-6

Library of Congress Cataloging-in-Publication Data
Campayo, Ramón, 1965-
    Maximize your memory / by Ramón Campayo
        p. cm.
    Includes index.
    ISBN978-1-60163-117-6
    ISBN 978-1-60163-748-2
    1. Memory. 2. Mnemonics. 3. Recollection (Psychology) I. Title.

BF385.C26 2010-01-05
153.1'4—dc22
                                                    2009050338

Cover design by Rob Johnson/Johnson Design
Interior by Gina Hoogerhyde
Translated by Victoria Fontana World English only

Printed in the United States of America
IBI
10 9   8 7 6 5 4 3 2 1

ACKNOWLEDGMENTS

The presentation of this book arises from a true need, a calling on behalf of many people, many students and many friends, who are interested in my study and memorization methods. I would like to thank all of you for the splendid "pressure" you have put on me, thanks to which I am now sitting in front of the keyboard of my computer. I am taking those first steps toward writing this complete course, which covers all the necessary know-how to satisfy curious readers, beginners and professionals alike.

So, you all form part of this book to a certain extent. I would like to return that favor by sharing with you the secret of all of our mental power. I hope that you will learn to use every one of our mental, active, and creative mechanisms to triumph in life, not only through the correct utilization of my study techniques, but also reinforcing your personal confidence and psychological preparation to the maximum.

I couldn't end this section without giving special thanks to María Jesús García, more familiarly known as "Chus," my wife, my friend, my partner, my secretary, my assistant....

I have been able to do so many wonderful things, thanks to her!

For her and for all of you, my affection and gratitude.

—Ramón Campayo
World Memory Champion and Recordman

CONTENTS

CHAPTER 1

THE MIND AND MEMORY

The Mind

This is the faculty contained within each one of our brain cells that allows us to think, reason, memorize, imagine, learn, feel, choose, etc. Because there is an infinitely greater number of cells in our brain than in the rest of our body, we get the sensation that our mind resides there, and this is correct to a certain degree.

The mind is complex. It has conscious and subconscious capacities, and, therefore, functions on these two levels.

We use the *conscious* mind exclusively for reasoning, choosing, and sometimes thinking (thought is mainly controlled by our subconscious).

On the other hand, different sensations control what goes on in the *subconscious* mind. This is where memory, feelings, and imagination mainly reside, which is why we are going to focus particularly on this area.

We can define the *unconscious* mind as part of the aforementioned subconscious mind, which is difficult to access. This is where past traumas are stored as defense mechanisms.

Memory

This is the mental capacity that allows us to store or retain information or a group of facts.

Memory is intrinsically related to the concept of learning—this being the knowledge and reasoning of that which is memorized.

Memory acts as a storage room (facts go in and out continuously) and, as I said before, memory resides in the part of the mind we refer to as the subconscious. Evidence of this is that everything we see or detect with any of our senses is unconsciously stored or memorized. We don't provoke this to happen, nor are we aware of it as it occurs.

At any time of day, we can easily remember what we have been doing during the last few hours, or even days, and we remember this with ease, because we have been memorizing these events as time has gone by. This is possible thanks to a totally unconscious memory process.

Another way of demonstrating that the mind's capacity to store data resides in the subconscious is how we are unable to control our memory under certain circumstances. For example, when we take important exams, many people suffer from a sort of cerebral paralysis, or mental block. This is caused by excess pressure and emotional tension, which can impede our memory (and other mental faculties) from working correctly.

If our memory were used and controlled consciously, we would never draw a blank, nor would it play tricks on us. How many times have you had something on "the tip of your tongue"? The harder you try to think of it, the harder it is to remember. Who hasn't been fooled by his or her own memory?

Because our memory resides in our subconscious, we will never be able to dominate it 100 percent of the time. However, with practice and training we will be able to control it 99 percent of the time.

Well, we know that the memory is a storage room that stores information. It doesn't matter if the information stored is visual, audio, or any other type of data. What really concerns us now is how to get the key to the storage room and, with that, gain absolute access to and control over this information. Thus, we are going to come to know its mechanisms, how it works, and the reason why it fails us at times. In summary, we are talking about getting the best performance out of memory and using it in the most efficient way.

Types of Memory

We can classify memory two different ways:

A) The duration of time we are able to retain memorized information:

1. SHORT-TERM MEMORY. For example: when someone tells us all the digits of a telephone number, many of us experience the following:

- If we don't jot it down immediately we will forget it.
- We are only able to retain the digits for a few seconds.
- Sometimes we repeat the number to ourselves incessantly, in order to hear it from our own

voice and thus remember it better until we can write it down.

2. MID-TERM MEMORY. This occurs when information is retained for one or two days maximum.

3. LONG-TERM MEMORY. This occurs when information is retained over months or years and only requires the slightest stimulus to keep it sharp in our memory. An example of this could be the city in which we were born, the image of a sibling's face, or our father's voice.

B) The senses are another way in which we perceive the information to be memorized. Therefore, memory can be:

VISUAL. The most important and powerful of all. Thanks to this, we can remember the things we see. A student reading a book can transform the written words into images, which we call photographic memory (not to be confused with eidetic memory). Individuals will develop a photographic memory if and when they have developed the necessary skills to do so.

While we are reading, a more or less logical series of links to all of the information we are reading is being produced. This is interpreted by the subconscious mind together with the data we had previously memorized or had already acquired in the past. We will refer to the understanding of the data, or facts, that the mind is able to retain or assimilate, as *learning*.

Students only learn when they are able to reason and understand what they are memorizing. This is only possible if they are working with what we will call sequential facts, which you will study later on. There are other types of facts (called pure facts) that cannot be reasoned and therefore cannot be learned, although they can be easily and deeply memorized in our long-term memory. We will also take a look at these soon.

Look closely at how we clearly distinguish between the concepts of memorizing and learning. Many people can memorize facts, but they may not even know what they have memorized, which means that they have not learned anything at all. In order to learn, you must be able to understand and reason what you have memorized, and also have a clear consciousness of these facts. The act of learning creates experience. That is to say, those of us who have learned something will be able to draw inferences from our knowledge in the future, at will, thus being able to make use of it. On the other hand, someone who has just memorized something without really understanding it will not be able to respond correctly when asked a question that is worded differently from how it was memorized.

Now I would like to undo the myth behind what is normally understood as photographic memory. Supposedly this is something that people possess, and with this they can magically, in the blink of an eye, "take photographs" of everything they see—for example, of a room—and retain a sharp image of this information in their memory as if they were really seeing it again. This is a completely false idea and nobody can do this, myself included, of course.

It is true that we all have the ability to create or remember small photographic "flashes." Although these only last a few tenths of a second in our memory, they can be developed with training. These make up the eidetic memory.

In any case, the strongest memories are those based on images, and even stronger if they are composed of moving images, which I call *mental video*. This is, without a doubt, the greatest weapon that all human beings possess not only for memorizing, but also for developing the ability to read quickly. For example, think about how well we remember information we watch on our home video or DVD. This is due to the fact that we are seeing these images in reality. So, being able to force the appearance of these mental images increases our reading speed, as well as our memorization speed, by leaps and bounds.

The rest of our senses can also help us memorize information, but these are really much less effective. Continuing with these senses and in order of importance, in second place we would find memory that works through hearing, which is called Aural, memory that we use very often every day and that allows us, for example, to memorize and remember a song.

Notice that in the first place we memorize, and then later we remember, which logically means that we cannot remember anything that we haven't previously memorized. Sometimes it can be difficult to remember something that we have already memorized due to certain subconscious censorship mechanisms that we have. These are really defense mechanisms that our mind uses from time to time (for some people, more often than they would like).

- *TASTE*. This is self-explanatory. Who can't remember the flavor of their favorite food? Especially when they are eating it again.
- *OLFACTORY*. Thanks to our sense of smell we can memorize and remember odors.
- *TACTILE*. Remembering sensations we perceive through our skin by touching something.

Finally there is another interesting type of memory that we call *kinesthetic*. This allows us to carry out all sorts of actions and muscular movements that we have already as-similated through inertia and unconsciously (for example, walking, writing, or driving an automobile).

It is very important for students who have to take *practical exams* to realize that the best way to develop this type of memory, kinesthetic memory, is precisely by practicing these activities over and over. Our goal here is to make them automatic, with little thought about what one is doing. And, why not have fun with it!

Memorizable Information

We have begun to discover the exciting world of the memory. But, what type of information is memorizable? What can we really memorize?

We can "only" memorize one thing: facts. Facts are the components of information, and the most simple information could be made up of only one fact. For example, if I say:

"The capital of France is Paris."

Here I am showing you a basic piece of information, composed of only one fact. I am giving you one fact about France, which is that its capital is Paris.

This information is composed of two parts (or focal points) which are "France" and "Paris"; and "capital" is a link between them. The link is the relation between the second focal point (Paris) and the first one (France). In this case, and as I have expressed this sentence, "France" is the source or origin of the fact (it is written first) and thus represents the starting focal point. Paris is the end or destination focal point of the fact.

Although it may seem the same, it wouldn't be the same to memorize the facts backward, changing the focal points and saying: "Paris is the capital of France." The starting focal point should always be the one that is of greater magnitude, and in this case France is greater with respect to Paris.

Therefore, the correct way to put these facts in order so as to memorize them better would be:

"France, capital: Paris"

This type of fact is really a pure fact (we will look at this more). Don't forget from now on that in order to memorize pure facts, it is always better to make the focal point of greater magnitude or greater importance, the source or origin of the fact. In this case, and as I mentioned before, it is evident that "France" is of greater magnitude because it is a nation and "Paris" is only a city. Therefore, whenever it is possible, we should memorize the information in the correct order:

Major focal point, link, minor focal point.

Observe and compare this order with the one we mentioned at the beginning when we said, "The capital of France is Paris." In this case, the information is more difficult to memorize because it appears as such:

Link (capital), major focal point (France), minor focal point (Paris).

If the order of the facts had been "Paris is the capital of France," we would have seen the minor focal point first, "Paris" as the starting point of the facts, and at the same time "France" as the end point. In this case, it would be better to change the order as I have explained before.

This may seem a bit complicated, or maybe strange, but it is necessary for you to understand it well and familiarize yourself with this in order to successfully continue on through the book.

NOTE: Keep in mind that the usage of the terms that you have read (focal points, links, etc.) as well as those you will read throughout the rest of the book (pure facts, sequential facts...), are my own coined phrases, which came about as a result of profound investigation. As they may be new to you, it is normal for them to seem complicated at first. However, they are very logical and well-founded, and you will soon familiarize yourself with them and feel comfortable working with them.

Types of Memorizable Facts

When a student starts to read a text, anyone can easily see that the information or facts that they are perceiving can be of two types:

1. Pure Facts

These are the facts in which there is no existing relationship, nor logic between both focal points.

For example, if a person wants to memorize all of the capitals of the world, he or she will see that no logical relationship exists between a capital and its country.

Why is the capital of China called Peking? What type of logic is there to explain that? It really could be any other city, right?

I could never deduce the name of any given country's capital by only using reason. If I repeat the name over and over I may be able to retain it for a few hours, or at most and in the best case, for a few days (very few days). However, I would finally and undoubtedly end up forgetting it or even worse, confusing the names of the capitals of different countries.

The facts whose focal points are not related in any logical nor predictable way, which we have decided to call "*pure facts*" (because they are purely and plainly just that: just facts), are predominately found on exams and tests.

They are also the most difficult to memorize for anyone who doesn't know how to do so. Just the opposite of what will happen to us.

We can unequivocally say that the density of pure facts found in one topic—that is to say, the quantity or proportion of them—will determine how "difficult" it is for a student (who doesn't know how to study) to memorize and retain the given subject matter.

Remember that for now, we are only testing the waters. For now, I am simply presenting these pure facts to you, but we still don't know how to memorize them. That will come later.

Let's take a look at the second and last type of facts we will find while we are reading, while we are studying, or while we are watching a documentary or a film on the television at home.

2. Sequential Facts

Among these there is a more or less logical and predictable interconnection, given that they follow a certain sequence, which can sometimes be easily rationalized or foreseen—hence the name—*sequential*.

For students, these facts make up the skeleton of all of the information in each subject matter. However, they don't delve into them too deeply, nor do they provide many details.

There's nothing better than a good example to help you understand what we are saying: Let's suppose that we want to memorize the movie (or the plot of) *Titanic*, whose information is equivalent to that of quite a large book.

I'm giving such a familiar example so that the reader can most clearly understand what we are talking about and follow along easier.

In this film numerous *logical facts* appear, which fall into more or less predictable *sequences*. To keep the terminology similar to this word, I have decided to call these *sequential facts.*

Among these sequential facts, some more logical than others, (some of them we can memorize easily because they are really predictable), we can say that in the first place, and at the beginning of the movie, *the passengers should board the ship*, and then, after a *luxurious journey*, the ship *crashes with an iceberg* (for example, logically, it couldn't crash with the iceberg before the journey began). After the crash, and only after it, is when *water floods into the hull.* Then *the boat will sink, the survivors will be rescued*, and so on.

Who can't figure out or predict the logical order of these sequences?

It is difficult to get confused or lost with these sequential facts because they allow us to easily infer the order of the film.

In other words: Sequential facts are those that we are able to tell to a friend when we leave the theater, after having seen a movie. In other words, all of the information in the film that has been unconsciously recorded in our memory.

As I said before, these facts make up the *skeleton of the information to be memorized* (or already memorized)—in this case, that of the aforementioned film. They will not give us the more intricate details, nor those that go beyond logic or reason. Nor will it give us arbitrary details, like the distance that the ship has gone or the number of victims caused by the shipwreck.

On the other hand, however, there are also many *pure facts* in the movie, which are not logical nor related with each other. For example, the fact that the ship that came to rescue the fading ship called *Carpathia,* the fact that the *Titanic* sank on April 14, 1912, or that it was an Irish ship (it could have been English, or from any other country, right?), etc.

These are examples of pure facts, or those that lack all logic and those from which we cannot deduce nor predict any other information. On the contrary, with sequential facts we can deduce that the ship can sink only after having crashed with the iceberg, and not before.

Among the most common pure facts that we find are dates, numbers, measurements, amounts, and so on. These facts can only be memorized by using a technique that employs far-fetched or improbable actions or associations, but students all too often use the ineffective technique of repetition to memorize.

The repetition technique for memorizing pure facts leaves a lot to be desired. We could get to an exam, for example, without being able to remember if the aforementioned ship sunk on April 14, 1912, or on April 12, 1914.

This type of terrible doubt could come up despite having reviewed and repeated the date over and over again, while memorizing the subject matter, and despite having memorized it "by heart." What student hasn't experienced doubts like this?

As we can see, using the repetition technique for memorizing pure facts also proves to be quite a drag. It's the same as repeating a date over and over again as if we were parrots, and as if that weren't enough, we could end up "drawing a blank" on tests or any time we try to recall the information.

Further ahead I will explain how to effectively memorize these types of facts in detail and with examples, which is through making far-fetched associations.

Now, tell me, what happens when we see a film once or twice? We can memorize the majority of it easily and without much effort, can't we?

So, the correct way to memorize a film (or any topic) would be to see the whole thing from start to finish, many times, not stopping or pausing it continuously, rewinding, or watching parts over and over again. This is what happens when students read a text (or one page) over and over again, incessantly rereading it. Wouldn't it be awful to watch a film this way?

Remember that studying should be like watching a film on your DVD player. Otherwise we are doing something wrong.

After watching the whole film, without interruptions, we will have a much greater understanding of its general idea, which will be the skeleton or backbone of all of the information that it transmits. This skeleton or backbone will be constituted by all of its sequential facts. There is no better way to memorize these than the use of repetition.

Of course, as we said before, the movie will also have a lot of pure facts, such as the names of the cities and people, dates, quantities, certain fortuitous or risky scenes, etc., which will have to be memorized separately with the technique of using far-fetched associations, which we will be studying soon.

Memorization Direction

Now, you are going to learn a general rule of great importance when it comes to studying, which you can use immediately:

We should always memorize from more to less.

This means memorizing from a greater extension to a smaller one, a greater range to a lesser one, getting the broad idea first and then zeroing in on the details.

According to the aforementioned rule, if we want to memorize a film, we should first see it from beginning to end, working with its complete extension first. It would be the same with a book or subject matter. I must insist. *You must study from more to less*, which is just the opposite of what happens with the depth and the detail of the film or book in question, which would progressively go from less to more.

This is all very logical, although when we first watch the movie it may seem that we lose a lot of details, don't understand them, or don't even notice them. However, we should still watch it from beginning to end without stopping because it will be more comfortable and efficient in the long run.

When we watch it for the second or third time, and we are quite familiar with it, is when we should take a more in-depth look at the details in the more complicated scenes.

However, this is something that we should do little by little. That way, we will progressively delve into the most complex and minute details, because we will be more and more prepared to grasp the increasingly complex information.

We can do the same with any subject matter. If we try to get a deep understanding of it from the start (instead of working with it first as a whole, more on the surface and only paying attention to the most simple details) we will most likely end up seeing it as more complicated than it really is. We may even end up feeling a little scared, or a bit discouraged. Furthermore, it would undoubtedly be much more costly to memorize this way. This is why we shouldn't worry if some facts don't stick in our memories when we read something for the first time.

Every student has seen how a lot of doubts they have while studying are resolved further along in the same chapter or in later chapters. They acquire more and more knowledge, and at the same time solidify and fill in the blanks of what they already know. The same happens with some film sequences we find confusing or don't fully understand. Often we end up understanding them at the end, but for the time being, so as not to lose neither concentration nor motivation, it is better to just let the things we don't understand go over our heads, not think about them, and just keep watching the film, right?

The whole point is to increase motivation and gain valuable time, which would be wasted if our student stopped too much time on every doubt that came up while watching a movie, or similarly while studying more profound or difficult concepts within the subject matter.

Therefore, we can see that if our pretension is to memorize a particular book or subject matter, we should read it as if it were a film, trying to see and hear the information that we are reading the same as we would with the scenes of a movie, without continuously going back over it. It would be extremely unpleasant to stop a film with the remote control and repeat each scene over and over again. So, the most important thing to do at first is to gain a full understanding of the general idea or framework of the information (sequential facts).

I must insist for the last time: It is better to see each topic or subject matter for the first time in its entirety and without going too deep into it. Then, each time you review, you will go deeper into it, as you start to get a grasp on the general structure of the topic.

When we watch the film two or three times, it is evident that we will have memorized its skeleton well. Nevertheless, we will not have been able to memorize its pure facts yet, which we will have to do through the use of far-fetched or outlandish associations.

You can see how everything I am explaining to you is innate in us and is directly related to our way of being and our behavior. In other words, I am not telling you anything that you don't already know deep down.

Memorization Systems

Depending on the type of facts contained within any information that falls into our laps, we can memorize them in the following three different ways.

Reasoning

This should preferably be used over any other type of memorization system. This method is employed whenever we are studying information that we are able to reason and understand. This information will be more solidified in our memory, and in this case we will also talk about learning.

Notice how learning has such a great importance on how we understand and answer questions that we see on a test. We have previously had to memorize and reason the information, given that our need for reasoning becomes much clearer in resolving and preparing for tests.

Reasoning is successfully used to memorize subjects such as physics or mathematics, for example, with their abundance of formulas, laws, etc. It is also useful in different types of subject matter that include facts that can be associated through a certain logic—that is, when learning facts whose sequences can be deduced perfectly by means of reasoning.

On the other hand, and also using reasoning as a learning and memorizing system, we can deduce new knowledge based on that which we have already learned and, at the same time, consolidate what we already know.

Logically, however, not all facts that we want to memorize can be reasoned. That's why we will often have to turn to the other two possible memorization systems.

Repetition

In the example I gave you of short-term memory, it is clear that what we are doing is repeating the phone number we were given over and over again and, if possible, aloud (in order to use our auditory memory) until we can jot it down on a piece of paper.

Repetition is the memorization system most commonly used by students. However, it is not usually used in the most effective way. We have said before that memorizing a subject or topic should be similar to watching a film at home on DVD, without interruptions. This refers to watching it in its entirety, placing the initial focus on the film as a whole. After seeing it a few times over a period of days, we will have correctly used the repetition system and have most effectively memorized its sequential facts.

Further along, in the chapter on subject matter preparation, we will take a deeper look at this type of memorization.

FarFetched Actions or Associations

When we see something very interesting, some action that powerfully attracts our attention, something that is completely not normal and that seems incredible to us, what happens?

What happens is that these extraordinary facts that we see powerfully attract the attention of our subconscious and will remain firmly engrained in our long-term memory.

For example, if we suddenly saw our dog start to juggle three oranges, wouldn't we remember that moment forever? Of course we would! And we would probably also remember everything that happened that day. We could answer any of the following questions without any problem:

- What were we doing before witnessing such an incredible scene?
- How did our pet catch the oranges in its paws?
- What did we do when the spectacle was over?

We would remember all of it perfectly, and for many years to come.

Memory based on far-fetched actions is considered the *most powerful of all*, due to the enormous part our subconscious (where our memory resides) plays in it, in order to store and not lose such special, unique, and "valuable" information. Hence, we shall call it *supermemory*.

CHAPTER 2

SUPERMEMORY

There are those who have already dabbled in making far-fetched associations or links because they have read about it in a book or someone has explained it to them. I won't accept this. You have to learn and control this technique perfectly and know exactly when, where, and how to use it. It is the most powerful mental weapon that we have.

In this chapter, you will learn the secrets that govern the world of the most impressive memory, used by professionals and also necessary for any self-respecting student.

With these memorization techniques, which seem to be authentic miracles for those who aren't familiar with them, and by means of some simple and practical exercises, your fluency and dexterity will improve greatly.

I sincerely hope you enjoy these techniques and learn to use them most efficiently at will, in order to yield the maximum while studying or doing any other activity.

So, with no further ado, let's take a look at the first initial recognition exercise.

First Exercise

The first exercise I propose, clearly demonstrates the great strength of our supermemory. This consists of memorizing a chain of 20 words after seeing them written only once. The first 10 words are as follows:

> tractor, light bulb, stork, button, table,
> skier, gorilla, ship, bicycle, bottle.

Memory can only work by means of linking. As for sequential facts, one fact leads us to the next through the use of a determined logic or sequence. If those facts are pure, like the 10 words here, there is no logic, and therefore we must create far-fetched links between them in order for the mind to regard them as "something unique." Only then can we memorize them automatically and effortlessly.

In the first place let's create a far-fetched link between "tractor" and "light bulb." Let's imagine, for example, a *tractor* that is on a field, and it is making a furrow with a plow that is connected to the back of it.

As the tractor goes along, the plow is digging up glass *light bulbs* from the ground which light up automatically.

Try to see this sequence of events as if you were only a few yards away from it. If you need to, close your eyes and make it as real as possible in your mind. Come on! Try to visualize it for a few seconds!

Continuing on, forget about the previous association, made up of the "tractor-light bulb" and let's continue linking the rest of the words with far-fetched associations.

The next word is "stork" and so now we must associate light bulb with stork. Let's imagine a *stork* hanging from the ceiling, with a *light bulb* in its long beak. Its long legs are hanging down and, if we pull on them, the light bulb alternately turns on and off.

See this image in your mind with detail. Look at the long body and feathers of the stork. When we pull down on its legs, we hear a "click" and we can see how the room lights up with a blinding light from the light given off by the lightbulb.

The two next words are "button" and "table." Now I propose a triple link with stork, button, and table. Let's imagine a *stork* that, like a riveter, starts hitting big black coat *buttons* into a wooden *table* with his beak.

He vomits or regurgitates the buttons from his stomach and they mysteriously appear in his beak. He does it so quickly that he seems like a machine. We can also smell the typical aroma of the wood.

The next word is "skier," and we have to link table to skier with a far-fetched association.

Let's visualize a *skier* in our minds, who is sliding down a ski slope, sitting on a *table,* which is turned over with its legs sticking up.

It is convenient to see details in the scene in order to reinforce our visualization: Let's look at the shiny, white snow. The skier is tightly grabbing the front legs of the table. He is going down very quickly, making all kinds of S's, and we see the snow-covered green firs pass by.

The next word we have to memorize is "gorilla." Now we will link skier and gorilla. This time we see a furious *gorilla* who rips out two bars from his cage and uses them as ski poles to push himself, *skiing* on two enormous bananas across a frozen lake. He is chasing after a polar bear who has stolen a bunch of bananas from him.

It is evident that with this association, seeing so many bananas will help us remember the image of the gorilla.

It is possible that the majority of you are thinking, "What a mental mess!" Don't think that way! Remember that our memory works subconsciously and we memorize automatically, almost without even realizing it. So, let's forget about all of the previous associations now. No "cheating" and no looking back, as it would be harmful. Get ready for the next words!

Now it's time to associate "gorilla" and "ship."

Imagine that the famous *Titanic* didn't really sink the way they have shown us in the movies: What really happened was, after the *ship* crashed with the iceberg, just as it was going vertical and ready to sink, a huge *gorilla*, "King Kong," came out of the sea. He grabbed the ship and set it back afloat. After this heroic act, he pounded on his chest with his fists. The passengers, frightened by the thundering noise, covered their ears with their hands.

Now let's associate "ship" and "bicycle."

We see one of those old steamboats, with a paddle wheel, crossing the Mississippi River.

The paddle wheel turns and drives the *ship* because there are sweaty passengers, as if they were galley slaves, *pedaling* in the hold of the ship.

There are two men helping them from the banks of the river, tugging the ship with ropes that are tied to their *bicycles*.

The last word is "bottle." So, let's associate bicycle and bottle. A cyclist puts her *bicycle* on the neck of a giant *bottle*, balancing and jumping on one wheel. Little by little, she pushes a cork into the neck of the bottle.

Are you ready now?

Good. Let me remind you that the first word was "tractor." Take as much time as you need to try to remember what happened with the tractor. What far-fetched scene did we visualize? This will help the next word to come to mind, and so on. Continue to do the same with the whole chain of 10 words.

Try to remember all of them before you continue reading. Go for it!

***

You were most likely able to remember all of the words without trouble and in the correct order. If you got stuck in any of the associations, you probably didn't see the far-fetched visualization I proposed very clearly. In this case, visualize it again, with more detail, or change the association for one that you like better.

Now take the last word of the previous chain, "bottle," and make a far-fetched association with the word "trunk." This is the first word in the new chain of words you will see coming up.

Then, link "trunk" with "bull" and so on until you get to "ball," the same way I did it before with the first 10 words. When you finish associating them all, you will have a chain of a total of 20 words in your memory.

trunk, bull, book, clock, rug,
cloud, door, rock, sea, and ball

When you have finished associating all of the words, think of the first one: "tractor." Try and remember all 20 in order.

I recommend that you write the words down on a piece of paper as you remember them, so you can check the results of the exercise afterward.

Hey! No copying or cheating! Good luck!

Mental Charts

A mental chart is simply a memory scheme that allows us to store information in our memory in an organized way.

The construction of at least one chart is completely necessary for any student. Furthermore, I can say without any doubt, that a student who does not have or does not know how to use a good mental chart will never be an efficient student.

Let's start constructing one quickly. The first thing we need to do is create a rule that allows us to *transform numbers into letters.*

Later on, we will make words with the numbers, because they can be visualized, and we then will be able to create far-fetched associations between them. This would be impossible to do with just the numbers because we can't visualize them if they are made up of more than two digits. This way we will be able to memorize all kinds of numeric data, measurements, articles, dates, etc.

Notice how, in order to do this most effectively, each number will correspond to one consonant (at least) of the alphabet, not to vowels.

I propose the following conversion (although each one of you can change it later for a different one):

1. **t** (easy to remember because the letter "t" is vertical like the number "1"). From now on, "t" and "1" should be the same for you.
2. **n** (the letter "n" has 2 legs).
3. **m** (it has 3 legs).
4. **q** (it can be associated with "quarter" or "quart")
5. **l** (it helps to remember that "L" is "50" in Roman numerals).
6. **s** (the letter "s" is the first letter in the word "six").
7. **f** (they look similar, don't they).
8. **g** (they also look similar and eight is the only number in the list with a "g" in it)
9. **b** (turn the number "9" around and you have "b")
10. **r** (The word "zero" has a "z," which is not a common letter at all and will be assigned to number 6, which leaves the "r" as the consonant of choice).

Good! Now take a few seconds to become familiar with the conversions above and memorize them.

***

The alphabet has other consonants that we will distribute among the numbers above, in order to help make our system as flexible as possible.

The *final conversion* of the numbers into letters, which you should memorize by heart, remains as follows:

1. **t, d** (easy to remember because "t" and "d" are phonetically similar)
2. **n**
3. **m**

4. **q, c, k** ("q" isn't so common, so we will associate "c" and "k" because they sound the same)
5. **l**
6. **s, z** ("z" is also quite similar to "s")
7. **f**
8. **g, j** ("g" and "j" also sound the same)
9. **b, p, v, w** ("b" and "p" are phonetically similar, and "v" because it rhymes; the "w" can be associated with "v")
10. r

The letters **"h," "y"** and **"x"** are not included in this chart, and can be used as wild cards that you can add as needed to form a word, just like the vowels.

Take as much time as you need to memorize the conversion of the chart by heart, before you continue reading on. It will only take you a few seconds.

***

Now we have a complete system that we can use to transform numbers into words. These words will be easy to visualize and associate using our far-fetched associations.

For example, if we are studying, and we come across a number, let's say **6409**. We can substitute this with the word "screw." We can add the vowels we need at our own discretion in order to create the word in question. Check and see if the consonants in the word "screw" make up the number 6409.

Now, all we have to do is create a far-fetched association between the word we have created, "screw," and what the number represents, just like we did earlier with the chain of 20 words.

We can remember all kinds of figures with this system: dates, telephone numbers, articles, laws, codes, valences and atomic numbers of chemical elements, physics constants, weights and measures, distances, formulas, and the list goes on.

Let's say that we want to memorize the telephone number of our local hospital. This number could be, for example, **329 1156.**

We can easily separate it into two words: **"moon"** and **"bottles."** Now we will make a far-fetched association. In this case we could make a triple link:

Imagine a *hospital* where all of the patients are in their beds. You can see the *moon* shine through their windows. The patients are shaking champagne *bottles*. The corks shoot out of the bottles with so much force that they hit the moon, creating tons of craters.

You have to imagine this far-fetched association as clearly as you can. You also have to hear the noise that the corks make when they shoot out of the bottles, as well as the explosions that they create when they so violently hit the moon.

When we think about the hospital, we will think of the moon shining in the windows and the patients shaking the bottles, and immediately be reminded of the corks hitting the moon. So, we will easily remember the key words: "moon" and "bottle," which, together, make the telephone number of the hospital in question, which is where the far-fetched association that we created, began (the starting focal point).

I suggest you do the next exercise to help you gain agility and fluency converting numbers into letters. Follow the example you have just seen.

Second Exercise

Memorize the following telephone numbers, as you already know, by transforming the numbers into words, and then creating far-fetched associations between them:

a) Work: 690 4356

I advise you to write the numbers in question and their associated letters on a piece of paper, so that it is easier to make the transformation. Do it this way:

6	**9**	**0**	**4**	**3**	**5**	**6**
S	B	R	Q	M	L	S
Z	P		C			Z
	V		K			
	W					

This way, you can take one letter from each column (only one letter) and it will be much easier to see the word (or words) you can form to substitute the numbers. For example, I can already see the word "shower" with the numbers 6, 9, and 0. Remember that "h" is a letter we can use as a vowel.

You will have to keep looking to find another word to substitute the numbers 4, 3, 5, and 6. How about "camels"?

Imagine you have a "shower" in which the water comes out of the humps of two "camels," one on each side. You will have to find a way to make it far-fetched, so that the result of the triple link you end up with (which will help you remember this telephone number) is something that really grabs your attention and keeps you from getting confused—something that would be impossible to forget if it really happened.

Do the same with the following telephone numbers:

b) Bus station: 786 5209

c) Train station: 455 4975

d) Airport: 365 1230

e) Theater: 934 6238

It may be difficult to find a word, but this won't happen once we have created our mental chart. You will always be able to turn to it in case of an emergency.

Creating Our Mental Chart

Each one of the boxes (or cells) that we create as we complete our chart should be represented by the name of an object, which can be easily visualized.

This object must contain letters that follow the rules that we have previously established for converting numbers into consonants.

So, for box number one, we will need the name of an object (objects are much easier to visualize than other words) that contains only one consonant, the letter "t" or "d." The number of vowels needed is indifferent because we can add these as we need them in order to give each box the name of an object.

Likewise, in order to create box number 56, for example, we would need a word that contains consonants "l" and "s," or "l" and "z," respectively.

Notice how the word "lease" could work perfectly in our scheme.

Remember that *you can add vowels at your own discretion.*

Let's continue on and make our own mental chart with 100 boxes.

The chart should be very personal, and the words you choose have to be objects that are all very different from each other and that you feel comfortable with. Apart from objects, we can also use people and animals, because they can be visualized perfectly.

Normally you will find different options for each box. You should choose one of the objects that I propose or create your own according to the rules that we have established, or, if you like, according to the rules that you yourself create.

Here are the *names of the objects* that we could use to make up the first 10 boxes of our chart:

1. Tea, toe, doe
2. Noah (boarding the animals on his arc)
3. Home
4. Hook, ice, key
5. Oil, loo
6. Sea, shoe
7. UFO
8. Guy, hag
9. Ape, bee, bay
10. Tree, door

Notice again that if you have a silent letter, like "h" at times, we can use it like a vowel, at our own discretion.

You should also include a **box 0: ear** (which is also round like the zero, and therefore easy to remember). Notice how the word "ear" only contains one consonant, r, which is the letter that we have associated above with the number 0.

Now memorize these first 10 boxes that we have just seen. It's easy.

Let me remind you that you should only choose one word per box, whichever you like more or is more meaningful to you. The words that you finally decide on for each box must always be the same.

Also remember that if you don't like any of the objects that I have given, you can choose another one, as long as it is consistent with the same rules of association (number/consonant) that I have presented to you (or the ones you design yourself).

Third Exercise

Using the far-fetched association system, memorize the following nine objects in order:

1. shoe
2. telephone
3. radio
4. newspaper
5. street lamp
6. candy
7. book
8. bed
9. car

For example, if you have used the word "tea" for the first box, you should associate "tea" and "shoe" with a far-fetched association.

Imagine a man who is walking barefoot with two giant, sopping *tea* bags under his feet as if they were *shoes*. As he walks on them the excess tea squirts out the sides.

If you used the word "doe" for the first box, you would have to associate "doe" with "shoe" with a far-fetched association. For example, you could do it like this:

Imagine you are in a forest, and you see a beautiful doe in the distance, in a shallow pond, drinking. As you walk closer, the doe starts to walk out of the water, and you see that it has four enormous clown shoes, one on each hoof. You can imagine its clumsy walk and water splashing all over as it steps.

You must then associate "Noah" (or whatever word you chose to represent the second box) with telephone.

Remember that the idea is to create far-fetched or outlandish associations. You have to imagine something that really grabs your attention: something that makes you laugh or feel, something that really impresses you, etc.

Keep memorizing the rest of the words in the exercise in the same manner. When you have finished associating the nine words, each one in its box, come back to this spot.

***

What? You've finished already? How did you do?

Now try to remember the whole exercise out of order. Notice how it doesn't really matter what order you go in if you use your mental chart. All of the information in it is already organized and in order, so it is impossible for you to get lost.

For example, answer the following:
- Which word is in seventh place?
- **In second place?**
- **In fourth place?**
- **Which place or box is the word "street lamp" in?**
- **And the word "candy"?**
- **And the word "radio"?**

If you make a mistake, either you haven't made a correct far-fetched association, or you haven't visualized it clearly enough in your mind.

𝒥ourth Exercise

This time we will memorize nine verbs:

1. eat
2. jump
3. laugh
4. draw
5. run
6. sleep
7. work
8. fight
9. swim

In order to do this exercise correctly, you have to associate each verb with its corresponding box number in your chart. Then, imagine each of the objects you have previously assigned to the boxes in your chart, performing the action of the verb on the list that is associated with its box. You can also imagine another similar action that suggests the one you have to memorize.

Don't forget to also visualize other objects that can help you reinforce the scene in your mind.

For example, in sixth place we have the word "sleep." Supposing that your key word for box number 6 is "sea," you could imagine something like this: Imagine an immense *sea* and all of its waves moving up and down, the reflections of light on the water witnesses to its movement. Then suddenly, the sea is tired, tired of moving, and just relaxes its waves. The sea *sleeps* and there is now what looks like a smooth coat of glass on its surface. There is no longer the noise of the waves. Everything is frozen in time and *the sea sleeps*.

Try to "see" and "hear" this far-fetched association with as much detail and realism as you can.

If you make a mistake, either you haven't made a correct far-fetched association, or you haven't visualized it clearly enough in your mind.

Fifth Exercise

Next, we are going to memorize, in order and with the help of our chart, nine words that cannot be visualized:

tenderness, sorrow, marvelous, strict,
friendship, cold, funny, blue, appetite

In this case, we should substitute these words for either objects or actions that remind us of them or make a strong suggestion to them, and that we can, of course, visualize. For example: *Tenderloin* can substitute tenderness, and then we can associate "tea-tenderloin," or associate whatever object you have chosen to represent box number 1, with tenderloin.

For the word *sorrow*, we could imagine the verb cry, or maybe visualize a noun that sounds similar.

For *marvelous*, something that is marvelous to us.

For *strict* we can imagine a *strip-tease* on ice or related to whatever we have representing box 4 in our chart.

- A good friend of ours for *friendship*.
- An iceberg or an ice cream for *cold*.
- A clown for *funny*.
- The sky for *blue*.
- A huge sub sandwich for *appetite*.

After making the nine associations, we will be able to remember, in each box, the object or action that substitutes each of the intangible words from the exercise. We shouldn't have any problem then recalling the original words immediately after, and thereby completing the exercise correctly.

If you make a mistake, remember: Either you haven't made a correct far-fetched association, or you haven't visualized it clearly enough in your mind.

Now we are going to *expand our chart* with 10 more new boxes:

11. Tit, toad
12. Dune
13. Dame, atom
14. Taco, dice
15. Tail, idol (you can visualize your idol)
16. Daisy
17. Tofu, thief
18. Dog, toga
19. Tape, tube, tuba
20. Nero (imagine him violently ruling his empire)

Sixth Exercise

Next we will do another practical exercise that will be useful for memorizing pure facts: the atomic numbers of 10 chemical elements. We will use our mental chart to do this.

Element/Atomic #
- Carbon: 6
- Nitrogen: 7
- Sodium: 11

- Fluoride: 9
- Aluminum: 13
- Phosphorus: 15
- Magnesium: 12
- Sulfur: 16
- Beryllium: 4
- Lithium: 3

Notice how, by using our mental chart to memorize in this exercise, we will always have a good visual image of at least one part of the association, because half of each association (in this case, the atomic number) is a figure that will correspond with one of the boxes in our chart, and therefore the object we have placed in that box. So, if the atomic number were 6, we would visualize a sea (box 6), a UFO if it were 7, and so on. In other words, half the work is done for us.

The other half of the association, in this case, is represented by *chemical elements*. Some of these can be easily visualized—aluminum, for instance. We could probably imagine the aluminum foil that we so often use to wrap sandwiches. We could even envision the sandwich itself. The same thing happens with phosphorus (a match). However, we will have to imagine other chemical elements indirectly, using some object that reminds us of them. For example, for fluoride we could see a tube of toothpaste instead (given that there is fluoride in toothpaste), or even a toothbrush. It would also help us to visualize the action of brushing our teeth.

For the rest of the chemical elements that we cannot visualize—lithium, for example—we will have to substitute them by objects that have a similar spelling or that remind us of them or help us remember them in some way.

Pay attention here! The word "lithium" would have to be substituted with an object (we should always use objects, because they are easier to visualize) with a similar name or whose name begins with the same letters as "lithium," and "cues" us to remember this chemical element—for example, the word "litigation."

When looking for a word to substitute another word that is difficult to visualize, it is always preferable to choose one that "cues" us to remember it by having the same first letters, rather than one that is only similar or rhymes with it.

For example, suppose that we want to remember the name of actor Marlon Brando, and it is on the tip of our tongue, but we just can't remember it. It will be easier for us to remember it if someone cues us by saying (or whispering) the first letters of the actor's name.

So, if they said: "It begins with Mar...," we would immediately respond: "Marlon Brando!" On the other hand, it would be much more difficult to remember if they only said: "His name sounds like melon."

This is why, whenever possible, we should choose a substitute word that cues us to remember the word in question, by guiding us with the first letters that both words have in common.

In this exercise, taking that rule into account, it would be better to use the word "litigation," given that it is easier to visualize (a lawyer in a courtroom). We can make a far-fetched association between this and the word "home," given that it is the word in the box in our chart that corresponds with the atomic number of lithium, number 3. This, I am sure, you can do without any difficulty.

Now, get to work on this exercise!

Remember that just making the far-fetched associations alone is magnificent exercise for your brain.

The Complete Mental Chart

Here I have provided you with the rest of the basic mental chart, in its entirety and with precise explanations for each word choice. You should know this chart like the back of your hand.

Normally, we won't use the "0" box, which we have established as **EAR**. We will reserve it as a special help box.

Each one of your boxes has to be perfectly clear. Choose only one of the proposed options for each box, or, as I have said before, you can create your own word according to the rules we have established or according to those that you establish and set.

Remember that it is much better to choose objects that can be perfectly visualized or that provide a clear and sharp image. Avoid choosing objects that are similar to other objects assigned to other boxes, which, due to their similarity, could create confusion. For example, "cup" and "vase" are too similar to use both in boxes 49 and 96, respectively, so you would have to choose another word for one of these boxes.

To make it more comfortable for you here I give you **the whole mental chart**, 100 boxes, with some of the possible alternatives to choose from:

1. Tea, toe, doe
2. Noah (boarding the animals on his arc)
3. Home
4. Hook, ice, key
5. Oil, loo
6. Sea, shoe
7. UFO
8. Guy, hag

9. Ape, bee, bay
10. Tree, door
11. Tit, toad
12. Dune
13. Dame, atom
14. Taco, dice
15. Tail, idol (you can visualize your idol)
16. Daisy
17. Tofu, thief
18. Dog, toga
19. Tape, tube, tuba
20. Nero (imagine him violently ruling his empire)
21. Hand, note (musical)
22. Neon, onion, Nana (what some call their grandmother)
23. Nemo (captain of the submarine, Nautilus, in *Twenty Thousand Leagues Under the Sea*), enema
24. Inca, oink (you can visualize a pig)
25. Nail, Nile (I can see it with the pyramids)
26. Nose, noose
27. Info (imagine an information desk)
28. Enjoy (imagine enjoying yourself in a theme park or something similar)
29. Nova (supernova), nap
30. Moor
31. Mote, meat
32. Moon, mine
33. Mime, Mom (don't use "Mom" if you already have "Nana" in box 22)
34. Mice, mocha
35. Mule, mile
36. Maze, muse
37. Mafia (imagine a typical gangster with his pinstripe suit and scarred face)

38. Mug
39. Mop, map, amoeba
40. Car, core (imagine an eaten apple)
41. Coyote
42. Cone, coin
43. Cameo
44. Cocoa
45. Koala, coal
46. Case, cheese
47. Chef, café
48. Cage
49. Cup, cape, cube, cow
50. Elixir
51. Lot (parking), lead (pipes), LED (imagine a digital calculator or watch)
52. Lion, line
53. Lime, Lama (imagine the Dalai Lama or a Tibetan monk)
54. Lake, yolk
55. Hill, hall
56. Lease
57. Elf, leaf, loaf
58. Leg, log
59. LP, lap, lava
60. Sire (king)
61. Soot, seat
62. Sun
63. Sumo (imagine a wrestler)
64. Sauce, sheik
65. Soil, soul
66. Ass, Aussie (visualize a kangaroo)
67. Sofa

68. Sage
69. Show, soap, soup, asp
70. Fairy, fire
71. Foot, fat
72. Fan
73. Fame, foam
74. Face
75. Flea, foil, flu
76. Fish
77. Huff (imagine the wolf from the *Three Little Pigs*), fife (small flute)
78. Fog
79. FBI (imagine the typical jackets with the initials "FBI" on the back)
80. Gear
81. Goat, guide
82. Jean, gun
83. Gem, gum, game
84. Juice
85. Igloo, gel, glue
86. Gauze, goose
87. Goofy (imagine the famous cartoon dog)
88. Egg, gauge
89. Jeep, jab, job
90. Bear, beer
91. Boot, bat
92. Piano, pan
93. Pony, boom (an explosion)
94. Bike, book
95. Owl, wool
96. Vase, visa
97. VHF (imagine a television)

98. Bag
99. Baby, Pope
100. Diarrhea, terra (imagine the red clay earth)

Mental Chart Expansion

Our mental chart may end up too small for us in the future. For example, the Spanish Constitution has 169 articles. If we wanted to memorize all 169 articles in the Spanish Constitution, we would see that we need 69 more boxes for the articles whose number exceeds 100.

Nevertheless, we can easily expand our mental chart as we need. Here are two possible ways to do this:

1) The same way we have seen until now, according to the rules we have set for building our 100-box mental chart.

For example, for box 101 we need:

T	T
R	
D	D

We can see that the word "Tart" works well with this model and therefore is valid for this box. We could also use "Dart."

For box 102 we could use "train;" "drum" for number 103; and so on.

Because this expansion method requires more work and time dedication (contrarily, it is also the most direct and effective), I recommend that, if you do decide to use it, you expand your basic 100-box chart only as you need to do so.

2) By means of wild-card situations, which will allow us to multiply it (rather than expand it). This means that each wild-card situation will give us 100 new boxes.

With this system, the chart quickly takes on enormous dimension, although nothing comes without a price, logically. In this case, any far-fetched association we make will be tripled, because on one hand we'll have the basic box (between 1 and 100), and on the other we'll have whatever we are going to put in that box and, finally, the wild card situation, which will tell us in which hundreds place we are in (100, 200, 300, and so on).

For example, suppose that we want to memorize article 149 of the Spanish constitution. Let's also suppose that your box number 49 is "cup," and that your first wild-card situation (the scene or place where your far-fetched associations take place) is an Olympic pool.

The aforementioned article deals with:

"The exclusive competences of the state."

In order to memorize an article, the first thing we need to do is read it and understand it, for which we must try reasoning.

Notice how it is not difficult to deduce that this article will only make reference to matters that depend on the state, not on the autonomous communities or municipalities. In other words, it only refers to the national government. Once we have read it, we find that it does indeed deal with what I have just mentioned. Thanks to our sense of reasoning, we won't have any problem figuring out the general idea of the article.

We may have to read it a few times and make some far-fetched associations within it, if it is broken down into points or different sections. In this case we would make a small chain (as you already know how to do) to memorize them. We would do the same thing with any other pure fact contained within it. Once we have done this, our only difficulty, and what is really quite difficult (so as not to say impossible) for any student, would be to memorize and then remember that all of this information precisely belongs to article 149, and not, for example, to article 125.

So, in order to do this, we have to make a triple association by linking the following factors:

- **"Cup,"** which tells us that we are dealing with article number 49 or that the article ends in 49 and belongs to a higher number in the hundred's place—149 or 249, for example.
- **"Exclusive competences of the state."** In this case we would have to visualize something that suggests this phrase to us. I imagine the president of my country, who wants to possess something for himself and only for him.
- **"Olympic pool,"** where the far-fetched action will take place.

Finally, all we have to do is unite all of the above in an extraordinary way, and have fun with it! We could imagine the following scene, for example.

I visualize the aforementioned *president*, with a large *cup* in his hand, trying as hard as he can, with the cup, to empty the enormous *Olympic-sized pool* that is replete with water. Every time someone comes near him, he hugs the cup possessively because he doesn't want anyone to help him or take the cup away from him. He wants to empty the pool *exclusively*.

You could also visualize him with his most important ministers (his state cabinet), each carrying a cup and emptying the pool all together.

As you can see, it's not only not difficult to study this way—it is also pleasant and tremendously effective. When you think about article 149, a cup and an Olympic pool will come to mind. You will immediately see that the cup is used to empty out the pool, and who better than the president (or his cabinet) to do so? And there he is, ready for action, possessively working away.

Likewise, if they ask you about the "exclusive competences of the state" on a test, you would envision the president in the aforementioned scenario. Notice how, in this case, it would be a bit more difficult to recall the article number. This is due to the fact that we would be starting from the far-fetched action, not from the box number in the chart. In this case, this action carried out would be the starting focal point in the association, and the article number (the box) would be the end focal point.

Remember the theory we explained about the focal points of pure facts? When we use the mental chart, it will be easier to remember the association order if you first visualize the box itself (the starting focal point) and lastly the object that we have put in that box (the end focal point). Therefore, it will be easier for you to remember the whole association if you are asked to discuss an article number. You'll go right to the chart and, in this particular case, immediately think of the cup and the pool.

In any case, when faced with the question of "the exclusive competences of the state" on an exam, it would be "cool" to start by saying: "Contained in article 149 of the constitution...."

Other Wild Card Situations

Likewise, you can create as many wild-card situations as you like. However, I advise you to create them as the need arises. Once you have created them and they work correctly for you, you shouldn't ever change them. In any case, for now it is more important that you dominate your basic 100-box chart as perfectly as possible.

For boxes 101–200 (inclusive) *an Olympic pool.*
For boxes 201–300 (inclusive) *in outer space.*
For boxes 301–400 (inclusive) *burning in hell.*
For boxes 401–500 (inclusive) *in your house.*
For boxes 501–600 (inclusive) *on a very dense planet.*
For boxes 601–700 (inclusive) *in the desert.*
For boxes 701–800 (inclusive) at *the North Pole.*
Et Cetera.

You can use these situations or imagine your own. As you can see, the only thing limiting you is your imagination.

There are other types of charts: *multiplicative charts.* These require a basic chart of at least 200 boxes, and the idea is to multiply both groups of a hundred to have a chart totaling 10,000 boxes. We are not going to study these because they require much more preparation on behalf of the student, and I prefer that you dedicate yourself, for now, to dominating all the techniques already contained within this book.

FYI

CHECK THIS OUT! IF YOU COMBINE A MULTIPLICATIVE CHART OF 10,000 BOX-ES WITH ANOTHER OF 10 WILD-CARD SITUATIONS, YOU WOULD END UP WITH A MACRO CHART OF 100,000 BOXES! THIS IS ENOUGH TO SCARE ANYONE. OF COURSE, ALL OF YOUR ASSOCIATIONS WOULD HAVE TO BE QUADRUPLE!

ALSO, JUST OUT OF CURIOSITY, I CAN TELL YOU THAT I PERSONALLY MANAGE MANY DOZENS OF MENTAL CHARTS OF ALL TYPES: BASIC, MULTIPLICATIVE, AUXILIARY, TREE CHARTS, ETC. THE LARGEST ONE OF MINE HAS A MIND-BLOWING 1,000,000 BOXES, BUT I HAVE NEVER FILLED IT (NOT EVEN CLOSE). HOWEVER, I DO INDEED HAVE IT, JUST IN CASE!

CHAPTER 3

PHOTOGRAPHIC READING (ULTRA-RAPID)

Why Is It So Important to Learn to Read Correctly?

First of all, a good reading technique will undoubtedly be a time investment with double the returns. In other words, it will give us the ability to develop a reading speed above and beyond the norm (at least three or four times faster). It will also give us the ability to memorize the information we are reading with greater ease, thereby considerably reducing the number of times we must review the material.

Secondly, with a little bit of training, **we will be able to memorize the information as we are reading it** because we will develop our ability to create a "mental video." This means that we will be reading the information so quickly and precisely that it will seem as though we are watching a film at the movie theater. If we saw this information in a movie, we would remember it much better than if we read it in a book, wouldn't we?

We will gain enthusiasm and concentration. We will be inspired by how quickly and confidently we advance through the text we are reading, while enjoying the sensation of our mental video.

Furthermore, it is much easier for the speed-reader to grasp the global idea of the information, allowing for a **much better understanding** of what is being read.

The greatest **DEFECTS** we find with the way most people read are:

Reading the words linearly without pausing to look at them for a moment. By doing this, we can't really grasp the ideas and information we are reading. If an object is still, like the lines of a text we read, our eye must also be still in order to perceive it clearly. We can't take a clear picture of a still object if we are moving the camera as we shoot, right?

The same thing happens with our photographic reading technique. We must look at a group of words at a time and "photograph" them by pausing for an instant. We must not resign ourselves to just scanning over them without stopping, which is how most of us usually read. This will only give us a jarred, fuzzy, and unfocused image of the words, making it impossible for us to see them properly.

Reading slowly. The average reading speed is approximately 200 words/minute, which:

- Makes us lose time.
- Makes us lose concentration.
- Hinders our ability to retain information, given the greater gap between each idea.

Furthermore, there are some students who, due to their erratic reading habits (reading back over the same lines time and time again), end up with a rhythm of even less than 100 words/minute.

In order to use our reading technique correctly, our eyes must move along the page with a **series of very quick jumps,** actually stopping on each one of the groups of words (within the same line) that we are going to photograph. These pauses should take between 0.25 and 0.75 seconds.

These pauses or stops—rather, these photographs—should be taken of groups of **four to six words**. Actually, when we read a sentence, we are not really interested in the meaning of each word in and of itself; rather, we seek the overall global meaning of the entire sentence together.

For example, if I say:

"The canary jumps and sings in its cage."

This sentence describes a scene in which we can globally visualize the actions that take place. Seeing it this way will help us to retain it better, because we are concerned with the meaning of the sentence as a whole, not with each individual word separately: "The... canary... jumps... and... sings... in... its... cage."

Slower readers have to consecutively add up the meaning of each word they are reading, which is done unconsciously, one after the other, until they figure out the overall meaning. This results in a reduction of both reading speed and concentration. These readers experience premature exhaustion because they have to look over the text six times more, and because they must make this unconscious effort to retain each isolated word in their memory, until they can link them together to derive the general meaning, also causing some mental tension.

Let's go back to the sentence: "The canary jumps and sings in its cage." If we read it word for word, from left to right (as everyone usually does), you can see how we would really have to make a subconscious effort to memorize each word we are reading in order to remember them. Notice how if we got to the word "jump" and could no longer remember that we were talking about a canary, we wouldn't be able to retain the whole meaning of the sentence, and consequently would not know what information is being conveyed to us. How can we memorize efficiently like this?

This sentence is short and easy to remember. However with longer sentences or more complex texts it is obvious that we could get lost (in fact I'm sure that we would get lost sooner or later). We would lose concentration and possibly even forget what we are reading altogether. It would be quite easy for our minds to "space out" and go off track.

This small effort of unconscious memorization, which I mentioned previously, might seem insignificant to some students. However, when we are reading sentence after sentence, for hours and for days, that small effort snowballs into something much greater and will undoubtedly hinder our ability to memorize the topic at hand.

While we are reading, at least until we get enough experience and fluency, we should **use a pen to guide us**. A pen, or other visual aid, will help us to focus accurately on the group of words that we want to read or photograph, and to keep a more regulated and precise rhythm as we read each line.

Using a pen as a pointer to guide us might seem unnatural to some readers, but I can assure you that it isn't. When we were beginning to read as children, our natural instinct was to use some sort of aid to help us read, typically our finger. Just like a viewfinder or scope helps us aim a weapon accurately, it is much better to use a visual aid when we read (facilitating our eye as it moves along the page) versus simply letting our vision float around aimlessly and imprecisely as we try to find the words or lines, and often lose our place.

Really, if we want to learn to read quickly and confidently, a visual aid is absolutely essential. It's not that we can't or shouldn't read without one, yet without it we will move along slower and with less precision and we will have to make a greater effort. Furthermore, it will take much more time and work to acquire a skillful technique, not to mention the disappointment that may be felt by those who only make it halfway.

We should not try to speak while we are reading, nor should we move our lips, not even a little. This will only slow down our reading speed. Also, we should focus our concentration and thoughts on imagining or visualizing what we are reading as if it were a film. This is one of the most important secrets.

The text that we are reading should be **positioned horizontally**, not on an angle (like we do when we write). This will foment faster eye movement. We should also read at a distance of at least 30 centimeters (around 12 inches) from the page.

The most significant **advantages** of reading correctly are the following:

This reading technique will help us improve our sensation of "mental video," which is undoubtedly one of the best weapons we have to help us memorize.

We save monumental amounts of time with a good technique. It would be like comparing a road trip, going a speed of 100–200 km/hour or (60–120 miles/hour)—in terms of reading speed, 100-200 words/minute—with a trip in a supersonic airplane traveling at more than 1,000 km/hour (600 miles/hour), corresponding to a reading speed of more than 1,000 words/minute.

It is possible to read so quickly because our mental ability to retain the facts and information that we are perceiving is much faster than our top reading speed. We are able to read 1,000 words/minute, but if we are watching a movie at the cinema, we can retain information and facts that would be equivalent to 60,000 words/minute, just as I have demonstrated many times and, furthermore, with even greater acuteness.

Because our reading speed is much lower than our mind's ability to record data, reading slowly will only decelerate our memorization process. Therefore, our reading speed must be brought to its maximum potential.

Is it really true that our minds can receive information at a rate equivalent to 60,000 words/minute and understand it all at the same time?

Of course it is. Allow me to show you. For example:

In a scene of a movie, we see that a man dressed in a black suit, who is leaning on the railing of a ship, is about to be murdered from behind with a huge knife, under the full moon....

Our mental absorption is so quick that we can take in all of this information in less than a second, with total clarity and an abundance of details: the reflection on the knife, the silence, the lights and shadows, the approximate height and other physical features of the characters, the speed of their movements, the music, background noises, etc. If we were to describe everything we had seen in that second, it would take us about 1,000 words to do so.

We have so much potential in this sense that we could even quite easily predict what will happen in the next scene: "Will this man end up murdered?" Or we might feel and think something like this: "Move already! You're going to get killed!" (This, of course, suppose that we like the character.)

Therefore, in one scene of a film we can grasp enough information to equal 60,000–80,000 words per minute. In other words, would need this many words to perfectly describe a scene of about one minute in length. In theory, this would be the maximum speed at which we could read, which in theory is much higher than in practice.

As we collect data at cosmic speeds through the use of the mental video that we all possess, we reach a maximum when we see scenes from a movie (apart from suffering, feeling fear, emotion, etc.). All of the information that we collect in just one second of that film, if written down, would take up about one whole page of a book.

Look at the short amount of time it takes us to watch a film (around two hours) and how well we retain the information that was conveyed in it. Compare that to how long it takes us to read a book. Furthermore, there is always less information in a book than in a film. There is no music, or anything of the sort, not to mention the fact that our interest, concentration, and other motivations are always heightened as we view a film.

Our data assimilation process is slowed down so much when we read, that is very difficult for our subconscious mind to connect all of the ideas that we have read in a text, hindering our ability to understand and digest all of the information conveyed to us on every page.

This is why I must insist that reading quickly and well will be quite similar to watching a film at the cinema, with all of the advantages. The trained mind of the speed-reader processes data so quickly that it will inevitably create a series of images, or at least sensations, because it is the only way to digest so much information in the given amount of time. There is no other way to do this—that is, without images at our disposal. This is a fantastic sensation and I call it *"mental video."*

Now, I hate to break it to you, but there are a few obstacles. Before an avid readers can create this mental video in their mind, they will need two things:

1) A reading speed high enough (at least 800 or 900 words/minute) to intake information containing a sufficient amount of data. Thus, the subconscious mind is forced to react by creating images in order to process so much information or data.

2) A trained and invigorated mind, so that you can assimilate the input of such a large quantity of information, so quickly, and thus create these images, flashes, or sensations (depending on the type of text you are reading).

In my presential courses, and after a 90-minute intensive training, I get most of my students to triple or quadruple their reading speed. After that, it stabilizes to around 700 or 800 words/minute, which is not bad for starters, is it?

I also work with them in order to "invigorate" their minds and open them in only a few minutes, so that they can receive and assimilate such a large quantity of information. Otherwise, they would read without understanding anything at all. Some of them really "flip out" when suddenly they can unconsciously and automatically see, feel, and hear the information in the texts that I give them to read. Unfortunately, for these gifted students, all the excitement distracts their concentration and suddenly the very same images that caused such excitement are lost. The students then read relentlessly in order to get that "video sensation" back. However if you want to achieve this right away, you won't be able to. The sensation only comes back when you relax and recover your technique. I gather that at mach 1 speed (around 1,200 words/minute) and with a little practice, there should be no problem achieving this sensation of mental video, which, by the way, can be trained by other means.

We are going to begin now with the first exercise. I'm sure you are anxious to get started. Some of the more complex exercises are not included in this book. In the future, I may write another complementary book in which we will take a more in-depth look at all of the techniques for photographic reading, mental video, and memorizing in general. However, this will be done when my enthusiasts are better prepared and have more experience thanks to this first book.

First Exercise

Next you are going to read two nice stories that are exposed vertically in thin columns. You are going to have to use your peripheral vision (out of the corner of your eye) in order to be able to see each whole line of text. Each one contains an average of only three words. The idea is to see all the words in one line at a glance. This is to say that you have to see the beginning and end of each line at once.

Attention!

Do not read from left to right. Read the whole line of text at once, as if you were taking a photograph of it. Then, making little jumps, carry on toward the bottom of the column until you have finished reading the whole text.

Make quick jumps and pause for a short time, an instant, on the line that you are reading (or photographing) in that moment.

Use a visual aid. You can use a pen or a pencil, and signal each line you read with it, so as to enable your eyes to move quickly and precisely down the page.

You should read at a rate of two lines per second. Have no fear. You'll see that it is quite a simple rhythm to keep up.

Read Text A first, many times in a row, until you can "see" what you are reading in your mind. This sensation is called "mental video." Besides having a very pleasant effect, it makes it possible for us to memorize the text sooner and better. It will also help you to concentrate better.

Read it faster and faster each time. When you have a hold on it and you can "see" what you are reading in your mind, start the same with Text B as well.

You can begin whenever you are ready.

Text A

One very
sunny day
in the month
of August
there was a
boy swinging

on a swing
in a park.
A very
well-dressed
man who
was also
walking by,
stopped to
look at him.
Suddenly he
left his briefcase
under a tree,
he loosened
his tie,
and sat on
another swing,
as he exchanged
a gleeful look
with the boy.
In the midst
of a hectic day,
the man
had found
a small oasis
of childish fun.

Text B

Led by
their guide,
the seven travelers
walked along
the white sand

beach of the
southern most
island of the
Galapagos Archipelago.
They were
searching to find
the nests where
the Pacific
green turtles
lay their eggs
and leave them
to incubate.
Every year,
in April or May,
the baby turtles
emerge from
their nests
and set out
on a frenetic,
life or death
race in order to
reach the sea
before the
birds of prey
turn them
into sandwiches.

Second Exercise

Check this out! The average reading speed of a university student is from 200 to 250 words per minute. From this you have to subtract the amount of time that is lost in going back an re-reading what was already read. After all, the average reading speed can be around 150 words/minute, or even less.

Now you have to TIME yourself. Pay special attention to the following:

- The two sample texts have around 80 words each, divided into 31 lines. If you read one text in 10 seconds, you would be reading photographically at a speed of eight words per second, which is not too bad for beginners. It is equivalent to reading at an inspiring speed of 480 words per minute!

- This should be your prime objective from the start. Start with "Text A." You have to signal each line with a pen, making sure not to make high jumps with the pen or move the pen in a curved fashion, rather just move it across, jumping horizontally and close to the text, smoothly and yet quickly.

- Try increasing your speed little by little until you can achieve your second objective, which is to read "Text A" in eight seconds. This will give you a speed of 10 words per second, or, in other words, no less than 600 words per minute!!! This is nothing like riding in a car now, is it?

- Then, you should do the same with "Text B."

These texts may seem quite simple to you, but this is precisely the idea. At first you have to begin with easy texts with very few pure facts that can be mentally "seen" without too much trouble. This is so that even the laziest minds (lazy for having worked in slow motion for so long) begin to hone their skills adequately.

Remember that we have already studied the three possible ways of memorizing. According to what we have seen so far, we can deduce that, because these texts can barely be reasoned, and they don't have any pure facts (or hardly any), the only feasible way to memorize in this case is through repetition. In other words, if we read them a couple of times, we are certain to be able to talk about them in detail. Logically, this system is the best choice here.

Don't forget that you have to try to mentally "FEEL" and "SEE" what you are reading. It's kind of like forcing your mental video to appear, which, by the way, is not the same as reading the text and then trying to go over it mentally by seeing the images. The latter, on the other hand, isn't a bad idea either; it is also good exercise. The mental video sensation runs parallel to the information that you are reading, at the same time, as if you were seeing the aforementioned film at the cinema.

If you are ready, grab a stopwatch and start reading the texts.

What am I saying, *read*?? *Fly* through them!

Third Exercise

We're going to take into account everything we have learned so far and start reading real lines. It's very probable that you have already practiced with an easy book by now.

Let's take another look at the texts you read before. You will find them on pages 62 to 64. The reason for this is simple: I want this exercise to demonstrate to you that the best way to memorize sequential facts is through repetition.

Notice how:

Each text that you are going to read is made up of seven lines of 11 to 12 words each.

On a piece of paper, and depending on the size of the line we are using, there will be a blank space remaining on the right, approximately one third of its width. We will use this space to write down the far-fetched associations of the pure facts that we come across.

You will understand this better in the chapter on the general study system, so don't worry too much about it for now.

The right margin should not be justified. That way each line and each paragraph will be considerably different from each other (photographically speaking). This will give you a great advantage as far as increasing your reading speed because there won't be any hyphenated words to make things more difficult. Furthermore, it is better for memorizing, because we tend to remember where certain information can be found in the text, be it at the end of a particularly long line, or in one that was shorter than the rest.

Now, grab a pen for visual support and get through each line in two jumps per second. In other words, you will be working at a rate of one line per second, which will give you a reading speed of about **700 words/minute**.

Time yourself and see how, indeed, it takes you eight seconds to read each text. You should read them as many times as you need in order to get these results. Don't worry if at first you go slower, because practice and reading every day play a key role in achieving this.

Remember that in order to *move your pen correctly*, you have to move it:

- Flat and close to the page
- Very quickly between jumps
- Stopping about half a second on each part of the line marked with the "( )" symbol.

For example:

" One very sunny ( ) day in the month of August ( ) there was a...."

Don't become hypnotized by looking at the tip of the pen. You should use your peripheral vision to take in half of a line each time, on each jump. The pen is an important helping tool for you to use, but the secret lies in forgetting about its existence, paying no attention to it, as if it weren't there.

Okay. It's time for you to get to it:

One very sunny day in the month of August there was a boy swinging on a swing in a park. A very well-dressed man who was also walking by, stopped to look at him. Suddenly, he left his briefcase under a tree, he loosened his tie, and sat on another swing, as he exchanged a gleeful look with the boy. In the midst of a hectic day, the man had found a small oasis of childish fun.

* * *

Led by their guide, the seven travelers walked along the white sand beach of the southern most island of the Galapagos Archipelago. They were searching to find the nests where the Pacific green turtles lay their eggs and leave them to incubate. Every year, in April or May, the baby turtles emerge from their nests and set out

on a frenetic, life or death race in order to reach the sea before the birds of prey turn them into sandwiches.

So, how did it go?

If your answer is *well*, then congratulations. You are reading 700 words/minute, three or four times faster than the average university student.

Keep using this technique when you read, especially with simple texts or those that you know already and are only reviewing. Evidently, for more difficult texts, you will have to slow down a bit at first, in order to understand them well. You may even have to stop completely to think, no matter what your normal reading speed is.

If your answer is *not so well,* don't worry, okay? We are here to help you. Read the line in three jumps, placing the support points like this:

"One very ( ) sunny day in the ( ) month of August ( ) there was a…"

When you are fluent enough, try to read each line in two jumps, but don't get overwhelmed by this now. Every day, keep applying all of the reading techniques that you have learned so far.

I recommend that you always read this way, no matter what falls into your lap. For now, don't worry at all about the reading speed you achieve, because, even though this sounds paradoxical, it happens on its own. Speed comes in time and with practice.

Next we are going to look at exercises that make up photographic reading training. Those of you who read every day using our technique will definitely notice how your cruising speed will quickly increase, especially at the beginning. Later on, this progression will logically slow down a bit, and then will eventually reach a halt, as with so many other things we do in life. However, students who not only read correctly every day, but train hard enough and are consistent, will delight in how much faster they progress, compared to the other students, and how the slowdown of that progression will occur much later on than if they hadn't trained as much. In short, you will be able to further increase your reading speed and quality, your concentration, and your reading comprehension.

Now it just depends on you and what you want to do.

Reading Training (1)

Many readers show great interest in continuing to develop their ever-so-important reading skills, getting the most out of their minds. Therefore, I am proposing a series of daily training exercises for you, so that together with whatever you read every day—news, books, etc.—you can achieve an effective and impeccable reading technique as soon as possible. You can achieve a very high speed that is comprehensive and at the same time is an important motivator for you whenever you need to use this skill.

You will find a total of seven exercises on the pages ahead. These begin with the fourth (because we have already done three) and end with the 10th. You should pay close attention to the first four exercises—that is, from the fourth to the seventh. The last three exercises are interesting, but are really more of a compliment to the others.

Do the next four exercises *every day*, for one month. The time you invest will come back tenfold because your reading speed will improve considerably.

I advise you to start with an easy book, one that doesn't have too many pure facts (dates, numbers, etc.) or one that doesn't require you to stop and reason out everything. A children's story is ideal to start with. Later on you can grad-ually increase the difficulty level.

For the sixth and seventh exercises, if you want, you can use a sheet of paper or small notebook to write down the dates you have done each exercise and the grade you have earned. That way you can compare them with other attempts and thus, evaluate your progression.

You can also use the book itself to jot down the dates and grades you get. In order to do this, use the diagrams that you see after each exercise.

This is the best option because you will always have it with you, and not chance losing it.

Before you start the first training exercises, you must take some time to learn to time your reading speed.

It's quite simple, but you must be a bit careful in order to do it correctly.

I do indeed hope that nobody even ponders the idea of timing themselves by counting each word they have read in a given amount of time.

The best way to do this, and also the fastest and most reliable (much more than really necessary) is by first choos-ing the right book (remember: easy reading) and then tak-ing the following steps:

1. Select four or five average lines and count the words contained within them. Calculate the av-erage, and this will be the amount of words that we will consider each line of the book to have.

2. Before choosing the average lines, you must select good possible candidates. To do so, you must select only full lines. In other words, don't choose lines that are incomplete (the end of a paragraph, for example) and also leave out any

lines that begin a paragraph, because these lines are also a bit shorter than the others due to indentation. Don't choose a line that has a particularly long word in it either let's say, no words that have more than three syllables.

3. We know that each average line can't contain any especially long words. But we also have to consider the short words, because all of them usually include very short words: "and," "of," "to." For maximum accuracy, I suggest that all of the words have an average of four or five letters, as would be the case in words like "line" or "drink." You could superimpose these words across a full line and then you would see how many of them fit in one line. This is probably the easiest and most direct way to find out.

4. Then, count the number of lines that a standard page has (you can also get an average number of pages if you find they are very inconsistent).

5. The only thing left for you to do now is, after reading, count the number of pages, and the number of lines you have read on the last page. Because you know how much time you have spent doing this, you will have no problem calculating your reading speed.

Fourth Exercise

The next text I propose to practice is perfect for what we are doing here. The text should not be too dense (it should have few pure facts) and should have good photographic potential.

You have to read it as usual, using a visual aid and re-solving each line in two jumps, unless it is still too difficult for you to do so. In this case you'll have to reduce the size of the section of the line you are going to photograph, and resolve it in three jumps.

Your ideal speed should soon be two jumps per line and per second (you might even achieve this after only an hour of practice). This will give you an attractive 720 words/minute (480 if you resolve each line in three jumps). If you are resolving it in two jumps, it is easy to deduce that you will be reading at an incredible rhythm of one line per second. Lawyers would kill to come even close to these reading speeds!

Remember once again: You should move the pen across the page quickly, with straight, horizontal movements close to the text. This is so you can take full advantage of every half second to truly photograph each part of the line that you rest the pen on. This also helps you avoid wasting time by flailing the visual aid through the air.

It might not seem so, but half a second is really quite a long time. Therefore, use it well and read fast, thinking about the reading and about the images you create of what you are reading. Don't think about anything else. I'm sure that you will really have fun with the text you have chosen.

Read it many times in a row and try to visualize what you are reading, as if it were a film. Also, after reading it two or three times, try to predict the information you are about to read, as you go, moving ahead in time.

Arctic Beavers

March came ferociously, hurling almost three inches of wet snow over the park, and then a nasty frost covered the

ground with a slippery glaze. I put on my tall snow boots and walked across the pond, knowing that the thin layer of ice would crack.

I sunk into the water twice, up to my knees. When I got to the burrow, I placed the birch branches on the ice, in hopes that a beaver would appear. Then, I sat and waited on a wet rock. Ten weeks had passed since the last time that I had seen a member of the colony. Had they stored food away for these rough three months? Were the six beavers in the burrow alive?

The wet snow began to fall. After a while, I heard a dull sound: A beaver had plunged through the opening of the burrow that led to the pond. He was just about to make a splash into the water, in front of me. A very drowsy-looking animal emerged. He floated for a few seconds, from one side to the other, and, after shaking his head like a dog, he climbed up a snow-covered rock about two yards from where I was sitting. He closed his eyes halfway and then did not move. I also remained still. After watching me for a moment, he proceeded to groom himself with his back paws. As I watched him clean his cheeks and rub his ears, one of the little ones came up to get some fresh air and sat next to him. Almost immediately, the other little guy emerged and lined himself up next to the thin dark-colored adult.

I was glad to see that both the little ones, born late, had survived the winter and seemed to be in good health.

Many days later, as I arrived to the pond, I saw that the ice had completely disappeared. The blue water reflected the sky perfectly. I was surprised to see how large the pond actually was, since I had only seen it in the confines of the snow and ice. In the meantime, the beavers were enjoying moving around freely, and I could now observe them at ease.

The first beaver to come out of the crystalline water was Laurel, who I hadn't seen for about four months. I recognized her immediately, despite the fact that she had lost the layers of fat that had covered her round body throughout the winter.

The Inspector was next to come out of the burrow. He and Laurel began to jump like dolphins over the back of their mate, entranced in endless aquatic acrobatics. They could dive in and out and enjoy a whole three and a half acres of water.

How did you do? Isn't it pleasant and simple to read like this?

Well, keep going with the rest of the exercises and keep up the enthusiasm!

Fifth Exercise

This time without a visual aid, move your eyes along the previous text. Do it **horizontally, vertically, and diagonally,** but always downward.

Mix the three movements and try to capture the largest groups of words possible. Your eyes will gain precision and independence.

Now try to capture groups of words from various contiguous lines at the same time. Start with two. Photograph them for an instant and then immediately look away from the book and try to mentally and precisely reproduce the words that make up each one of the lines, even if they are disconnected words to which you cannot give any meaning.

This exercise is meant to develop your vertical peripheral vision—that is, from top to bottom. We have already been practicing your horizontal, or side, vision continuously.

When you have been practicing for a few days, you will feel more comfortable with this exercise. Try to do it with three or more lines, or even lines from different paragraphs.

You could dedicate four or five minutes per day to this exercise. Really, it will be the first one in your daily series of training exercises.

For day two, and thereafter, look for a book that is *easy to comprehend*, as I have advised you before. If you want, it can be something similar to something you have read here. This is the best way to do all of the training exercises that I propose to you.

Sixth Exercise

Read *as fast as you can*, with a visual aid and **without worrying about comprehension.**

Do three sets of reading, one minute per set, resting 30 seconds between each one.

Time your reading speed and note it down in the graph on the next page.

Note: Don't worry too much about the short words like "of," "a," "to," and the like, which don't often have any use, much less worry about the commas or periods.

Neither punctuation marks nor these linking words can be visualized in our minds, simply because the possibility does not exist to do so. I can see "a yellow canary," but what I am really seeing is the image of "yellow canary"— only its image and its color. I can't see "a," "to," "of," etc.

The truth is, when we watch a film at the cinema, we don't visualize these linking words, commas, or periods either, do we? Nevertheless, this does not impede our ability to understand the plot of the movie perfectly.

DATE	SPEED	PROGRESSION	NOTES

Seventh Exercise

Read *as fast as you can* and with a visual aid, but this time, contrary to the last exercise, you should do it **with a full comprehension** of the reading.

In any case, you should not stop at any time. You should do the following:

1. If you think you are going too fast and you don't understand what you are reading very well, simply slow down your reading speed a bit.

2. If you think that you can go faster, because you feel comfortable with the rhythm, you are going, then raise the speed again, but without fear. Go faster or slower, as you wish, but don't hesitate to experiment with whatever changes in speed that you feel are necessary.

Do three sets of reading, one minute per set, resting for 30 seconds between sets.

Time your speed and write it down in the following chart. Good luck!

DATE	SPEED	PROGRESSION	NOTES

Ultra-Rapid Reading Training (2)

For practicing the photographic reading technique, and in general all types of mental photography, I often use numbers, including binary and decimal numbers.

As you know, there are world mental photography championships and they use these numbers to measure this capacity.

It is logical that they use these numbers for such competitive events out of fairness to all the competitors. If they used text, the competitor who speaks the language of the text would always have an unfair advantage.

Furthermore, it would be impossible to translate the text into every language. Its size, referring to the amount of words it has, as well as its overall extension (also influenced by the change in size of the new translated words), could become greater or smaller, sometimes decisively presenting new advantages or disadvantages to certain competitors.

We are going to touch on this discipline, although it does not form an essential part of the training dedicated to improving your reading speed and efficacy. These simple exercises are complimentary; however, they are also quite effective.

It won't take you long to do them, and I am sure that you will enjoy them. Whenever you are ready...go for it!

Eighth Exercise

You will see some numbers written in groups of threes following. You have to read them by focusing your eyes (without a visual aid) on the middle digit, without moving your eyes from that spot. Keep your vision focused on this number for half a second, before moving down to the next one, and so on. As you can easily see, you will be working at a rate of two numbers per second.

Make an effort to open your peripheral vision in order to take in and clearly see all three digits in each number. You will see that it is quite simple.

Do the first column on the left (it has more simple numbers), then the middle column, and finally the right column.

001	320	465
100	650	682
777	608	249
282	012	139
090	042	572
858	114	819
003	993	931
900	677	658

So, how did you do? Piece of cake, right?

Ninth Exercise

We are going to read the numbers from the previous exercise again, but now try to mentally repeat the number that comes before the one you are reading.

For example, imagine that you already have your eyes on the second number, which is 455, which I have shown in bold.

At this very same moment you have to be mentally pronouncing the number before it, in this case, the very first number. You are supposed to have just finished reading (or photographing) number "six hundred and eighty-six":

686
455
324
295

Likewise, when you read or fix your eyes on the second number (for about half a second), number 324, you should pronounce in your mind number 455, at the same time, because it is the number you have just finished photographing.

And so on, until you have done all of the proposed columns of numbers.

Notice how you will always be lagging by one number, and therefore, you will pronounce (in your mind, not aloud) the number right before the one you are viewing at the time.

It is an excellent exercise for photographic capture, and also improves concentration and makes it possible for our minds to be in two places at once, thereby increasing its working speed.

Practice it as many times as you need until you totally dominate the technique. I advise you to practice this a little bit each day, if necessary.

Tenth Exercise

Now we're going to complicate things a bit, but only a little. Next we will be working with the numbers that follow, which are a bit more difficult because they all have four numbers instead of three.

First, do the same thing you did in the eighth exercise. Do you remember? Do this without mentally pronouncing, just reading.

Then, read it again, but now pronounce them in your mind, with the one-number lag, just as you did in the last exercise.

0010	3200	4653
1000	6500	6823
7777	6080	2497
2828	0120	1396
0900	0420	5726
8585	1144	8194
0033	9939	9313
9009	6776	6586

If you want, you can try writing other, different numbers, and practice with them.

CHAPTER 4

GENERAL STUDY SYSTEM (R.C.S.)

Next, I am going to break down my study system for you. I call it the Ramón Campayo System, and it is, without a doubt, the most effective system that a student can find and learn. It is the result of many years of research on my behalf, and it brings together the many different tools and weapons that we have been learning or acquiring on our journey through this book. If applied correctly, the results are surprising, given that it is foolproof.

Initially, the *subject matter* is composed of a series of *content areas*.

These are, in turn, composed of *topics*. We can consider each topic as a basic unit of the subject.

The topics are made up of *chapters*.

The chapters are made up of *key points* that make up the framework or basic divisions of the topic.

These can be broken down into *sections and subsections.* And the last, finally, into *paragraphs.*

Of course, there are not always this many subdivisions.

First, we should take five or 10 minutes to look at all of the material we have accumulated in relation to our subject matter. This includes everything we have on the initial subject matter (books, notes, etc.), which I will now refer to as raw subject matter or base subject matter. We do this in order to get an idea of its difficulty and length, and to begin developing our summaries. Throughout this chapter, the word "raw" refers to the subject matter or its subdivisions that we have not yet sifted through, summarized or adapted for our study purposes.

Then, we should start by *reading a raw topic*, which will be one particular topic from our raw subject matter, normally at the beginning of our study guide or first on our list. For competitive exams this doesn't necessarily have to be the first topic. It should be the most generic, the least complex, the one we like best or that grabs our attention. It is always better to start with a good feeling.

Our study system consists of three clearly defined parts:
1. Personalization of the subject matter.
2. Memorization.
3. Review.

1. Personalizing the Subject Matter

Logically, we will go in order, starting with the first point: **personalizing the subject matter.**

We will start at the beginning of the INITIAL subject matter (which we also call raw or base subject matter), which is composed of the books and notes that we have available to us.

We have to transform this subject matter into something different and infinitely more effective, which will be our own *personal subject matter*. This personalized study guide will be composed of *special summaries*, which will be real study "highways," and of *mental maps* (photographic designs).

After reading over our first raw topic, we should then go back and read a key point from this topic (which, as we said before, on competitive exams doesn't necessarily have to be the first one). We will then begin *creating our summary*, point by point, changing the order of the facts and information as we see necessary or logical. (We might put facts found at the end of the raw key point, at the beginning of our summary.)

We can consider the key point as the base for creating the summary, and therefore we can start with whichever key point we prefer.

It is very important that our summary contains **all of the pure facts** from the initial topic. It is also important that, when you start developing your summary, you pay close attention to the main ideas, as well as the most graphic parts. In other words, put all of the most general information and that which we can somehow see "photographically" at the beginning.

As an exception, and **only if you do not have time to make the summary**, you could underline all of the important information with a green pen. (I do not advise using a highlighter here, as it is quite harsh on the eyes.) Leave out only the filler or impertinent information (if the exam is multiple choice). If it is an essay exam, only mark the most important parts, limiting and adjusting the information to fit into the time frame you will be given to develop your answer on the exam. Not many students realize how absurd it is to study extra information that they won't have enough time to expose on the exam. In either case, this helps us to considerably reduce the length of each topic.

It is also a good idea, if we don't have enough time to make the summaries, to write out associations between the pure facts in a separate notebook. You should also make a reference to the page in this notebook that the association is on, in the margin of the book you are studying (There normally isn't room for much more than this in the margins.) You should also mark where these facts can be found in the textbook with a blue pen, in order to later be able to find the pure facts in the blink of an eye.

The reason we use a green pen to underline in the book is so that we can easily and immediately distinguish it from the black text of the book and from the blue marks representing the pure facts and their corresponding associations.

Therefore, depending on the time we have, we can make our summaries or underline whatever text we desire in the book itself, again, adjusting to the time we will be given to discuss the topic on the exam. Also, studying for an exam and studying for the simple pleasure of learning are not one in the same, just like the study techniques used to prepare for different types of exams will be different.

Nevertheless, let's not forget that with a well-written summary, we will save a lot of time, not only when we try to understand and reason out the topic, but also when memorizing and reviewing it. Reading speed also plays a big part here, and I remind you that you have to read the summaries many times in order to memorize them correctly.

My last bit of advice on this, still assuming that we are really under the gun, would be to make at least a few summaries of some of the topics in your subject matter, particularly those you find most complicated or difficult. On the other hand, remember that you only have to make these summaries once. Therefore, if for some reason you don't pass the exam, you will have them already prepared for the next time you take it (try, try again), and then the preparation will really be fast and simple.

So, psyche yourself up and summarize, but only the way I show you. Forget what they have taught you in the past. This is your best bet for the future.

With our summaries, we will try to:

- *Eliminate all the filler* of the raw topic.
- *Use our own vocabulary* and express ourselves in our own particular way (which will help us memorize this in the future), as long as we maintain a minimum level of culture and preparation; and respect the technical and formal words we come across, especially in definitions.

We do not omit any pure facts from our summary. *We must include all of them.* In other words: our summary will contain the least amount of information possible, yet at the same time, with summary in hand, we should be able to answer any question asked about the topic.

We should also exclude all of the information we already know from the summaries, or any information that forms part of our general culture or knowledge, because there is no use being repetitive. We wouldn't have any trouble recalling this knowledge on an exam. Plus, we should learn to trust in ourselves completely. Eventually, all of the topics we memorize will end up forming a part of the inherent knowledge that we all have within.

With our summaries, we will be able to:

- *Reduce the size of the initial subject matter* to about half or less than half—sometimes even down to one 10th of the original.

- *Memorize the sequential facts sooner and better.* The facts in our summaries will be more familiar to us because they are linked to our own particular vocabulary and characteristic expressions, and also because we will have changed the order of the information in a way that best suits us, making it more logical and coherent.
- *Memorize the pure facts once and for all, with complete clarity, and furthermore, having a good time in the process.* We will have conveniently made all of the necessary far-fetched associations and they will now be written down in the margins of each summary, in plain sight.
- *Improve concentration* by memorizing the topics later on, because we won't get lost in the extraneous "filler" contained within the raw topics.

Creating the Summaries

This is not about summarizing to the likes of Tarzan. Rather, it's about using coherent words (from our own vocabulary) that link the facts in a logical way, in order to increase understanding. At the same time, you have to get directly "to the point." This is because normally the raw topics are too wordy and repetitive, and it is not necessary to read them and reread them over and over again. Hence, we should avoid this and stick to the important ideas.

If you are writing out your summaries with a pen, it is better to use notebooks with recycled paper. This way they won't get bent, and they will be better protected and easier to read in any position (sitting or lying down). Furthermore, we can take our summaries with us wherever we go without losing any of them. Most importantly, this type of paper doesn't make us as sleepy or tired as conventional paper, because it doesn't reflect as much light as white paper does. This will allow us to study longer, better and without getting so tired.

You can also find recycled paper in loose sheets, which logically have the same anti-reflection effect as the notebooks do. I prefer the notebooks, if I have to write it by hand. I find them to be more comfortable, although this is just my own personal opinion and should not influence you in any way. This really depends on you and what makes you most comfortable.

Nevertheless, if you have a **personal computer**, I suggest that you use this, and then print out the summaries on recycled paper or yellow paper. You will see the advantages of using a computer later on, in the section on "summary examples."

The lines of the text in our summary should be **10 to 12 words long** (see "reading techniques"). They should take up approximately two-thirds **of the width of the paper**, which will not only help us read faster, but will also provide us with enough space on the right margin to be able to write down our far-fetched associations of the pure facts.

Remember that **the right margin should not be justified** because this makes the whole text look the same to us. Furthermore, justification separates the words in a line, which creates a detestable effect for photographic readers because they can't capture or photograph as many words at a time, given all the white space in between. If we don't justify the right margin, on the other hand, and **we don't separate words with a hyphen** when they don't fit on a line (which also impedes our reading speed), we will find that working with a text that is uneven along the right margin helps us to memorize it photographically. This is precisely because the length of each line varies, making it easier to remember the information. This is similar to the photographic effect that makes us remember information better when it is next to something crossed out, for example.

The right margin, which will take up approximately **one-third of the width of the page**, should be reserved for writing our *far-fetched associations* of pure facts, which should be written after **a small symbol** that we shall choose specifically for this purpose. This symbol will help us to visually move faster between the pure facts written in the summary text and the beginning of their association in the right margin. It will also help us move faster along the associations we have written in the right margin, because we will know at a glance how many associations we have written and where each of them begins and ends.

This small symbol (I use a five-pointed star) will instantly indicate to us that there is a far-fetched association written after it. We should write these associations with a *blue pen*. We should also use the same color to underline or circle the key words of the associations in the right margin (where we have made the association itself) as well as in the summary.

Important: As we are writing the summary, we have to keep in mind that each paragraph should explain only **one main idea** and its secondary ideas, in order to memorize it better later on. Even if the raw topic isn't separated by paragraphs, we will do this as needed in order to adapt our summaries to this rule.

This will also help us later on when we make our mental maps as well as with an *occasional memorization* for emergency situations, by means of *associating the different key words that represent each paragraph to each other*. This will also be of great help if we have to discuss a topic on an oral exam or if we need to give a speech, for the same reasons I have mentioned previously.

Any figures should be **written numerically** (with digits) rather than with letters.

Any **doubts that come up** as we make our summaries should be jotted down on a blank sheet of paper or at the end of our notebook (writing from back to front) because these doubts can come up again later. This way, we have them together with the subject matter and they won't be misplaced. If we use a notebook, it's best to make a note of the doubtful situation and its solution in the summary.

NOTE: BEFORE CONTINUING ON WITH THE SUMMARY WE SHOULD GET THESE DOUBTS CLEARED UP BY A SPECIALIST OR A TEACHER. IF THERE ARE A LOT OF DOUBTS, IT WOULD BE BEST TO FORGET THIS SUMMARY FOR THE MOMENT (IF WE USE A NOTEBOOK WE CAN LEAVE SOME BLANK PAGES) AND START ANOTHER TOPIC ALTOGETHER. THIS IS ONE OF THE REASONS IT IS BEST TO START BY SUMMARIZING THE MORE SIMPLE TOPICS. IT WILL GIVE US A HEALTHY AND REAL SENSATION OF ADVANCING THROUGH THE SUBJECT MATTER QUICKLY, RIGHT FROM DAY ONE, WHICH IS QUITE MOTIVATING. FURTHERMORE, WHEN WE FINALLY DO TACKLE THE MORE DIFFICULT TOPICS, WE WILL HAVE ALREADY ACQUIRED A VAST AMOUNT OF BACKGROUND INFORMATION ON OUR SUBJECT MATTER, WHICH WILL HELP *US UNDERSTAND THESE TOPICS BETTER AND IN A LOT LESS TIME.*

Before starting to create our summary, we should try to **have all the information available right at our fingertips,** from every source that we are using, so that the summary ends up being the result of joining all of these sources together.

If we write the summaries in a notebook, we should leave **one or two blank pages** after each one, in case we come across any more information in the future that is worth adding.

The **best pen** for writing our summaries is a *black pen*. Just as I advised you to use recycled paper, this color reflects the least amount of light. This together with the paper makes the best combination for less light reflection, which will allow us to work longer on our personal subject matter, avoiding premature exhaustion often caused by an excess of reflected light.

Also, we will use a *blue pen* for the associations of pure facts, as you already know.

Blue text is relaxing to the eye. This is why we shouldn't use this color to write our summaries. It could make us tired too soon. However, it is *ideal for taking essay exams*, because seeing long texts in this color will produce a relaxing effect.

We should also use **highlighters**. I advise you to use three different ones:

- **Blue**, to highlight the titles of the topic, of the chapters, and of the key points.
- **Red**, to highlight the titles of the different subdivisions that make up each key point.
- **Green**, to highlight the titles of the new subdivisions included in the ones we have previously highlighted in red.

Careful! Only highlight *the titles of the parts of each topic*, never the text.

YOU CAN REMEMBER THE USE AND PRIORITY OF THE HIGHLIGHTER COLORS BECAUSE THEY GO FROM A GREATER TO SMALLER RANGE: FROM BLUE, WHICH REPRESENTS THE BROADEST AREAS (THE SKY, THE SEA, ETC.), TO GREEN, WHICH, BECAUSE IT IS THE CALMEST COLOR (NATURE, TREES, ETC.), WON'T PROTEST BEING IN LAST PLACE.

If some part of our initial subject matter is very complicated, even too much to summarize it, it would be best to forget about it for the moment, and frame it or mark it with a pen in order to find it easily in the future. (One of the advantages of the summaries is that we can do them in whatever order we like.) Nevertheless, **the most difficult topics should be left until the end**, because we will have them fresher in our minds at the time of the exam. Also, because we will have acquired more knowledge, having the rest of the subject matter under our belts, we will have no problem taking on the more difficult ones when the time comes. We will probably have even learned some specific information that will clear up another, more difficult topic, or at least help us understand it better.

Likewise, leaving the more complicated topics for the end also means that there is nothing to impede us from moving through the subject matter quickly, happily, easily, and with confidence, right from the start. This carries with it immeasurable **positive psychological effects**.

In general, competitive exam candidates have an advantage over students in any academic school year as far as the preparation of the personal subject matter. The former can study at their own rate, and thereby can relax more throughout the whole preparation process. On the contrary, academic students are obliged to follow a rhythm set by others, which can sometimes go too fast to follow or even too slow, depending on the circumstances.

We will make *Mental Maps* from our summaries, one per topic, and this will complete our personal subject matter.

The Adapted Subject Matter

On competitive exams that include or are in the form of essay tests, you should *ADAPT your personal subject matter,* near the exam date. This adaptation should result in reduced summaries, which take the same amount of time to write out as you will be given on the exam, as stipulated in the exam rules.

But why not just make the adapted version from the start? Why should we wait until we get closer to the exam date?

Because if, after all, close to the exam date, the exam changes from essay to multiple choice (because the judges exercise supreme authority, this has been known to happen and can happen again), we would thereby avoid the risk of not having memorized enough information to succeed on this new test. This would undoubtedly be the case if we only used a shortened version of the subject matter. For study professionals, like you and me, this is too great a risk to take.

Furthermore, shortening the topics for no good reason would also mean sacrificing the opportunity to learn extra information that the candidate may need later on if he or she took another competitive exam, on the same subject matter, that was composed of multiple choice tests or short-answer questions (these are answered with only a few words and therefore can be taken from anywhere). These types of exams require the use of a broader subject matter in order to prepare them correctly.

Remember: *With multiple choice exams*, the subject matter has to be as extensive as possible because we could be asked a question about anything, even the most minute details.

Therefore, as we have said before, if we create these adapted summaries close to exam time, we will also *develop more writing strength*, which will be very convenient on the day of the exam. Our hand won't get so tired and we probably won't get "writer's cramp." This is also useful for *rehearsing the presentation of each topic* on the exam, by carefully watching the expressions that we choose to use and our spelling, so as not to make mistakes. In general this will be very useful for organizing everything we have learned more effectively.

Because our personal subject matter will almost always be much more extensive than the subject matter adapted to the time given on the exam, we should choose only the most important parts (for the adapted summaries) and what we consider to be the most technical information. Then, we can embellish that information with what we like best or what we remember best. Likewise, if we need more information to cover the time given in the exam to discuss the topic, we should then look to expand on it. We should look for what's missing, using any means available to us: another student's notes, other books, etc.

I must INSIST on the importance of writing this adapted version close to the exam date, only after we have created and memorized all of our personal summaries perfectly, because:

- *It will then be easier to create*, because we will be experts on the whole subject matter and will probably have learned new information from other similar or complementary topics from the subject matter that have to do with the one we are working on. Thanks to this, we can add this information or even move it from one topic to another because it will fit perfectly wherever we put it.
- If the exam were to be changed in the last minute, from one type of test to another, like short-answer, for example, we would still have *complementary information* from our personal summaries fresh in our minds to help us answer.
- In the unlikely case that we couldn't remember part of the information that we had to discuss in an answer on the exam, we could always replace it with other information. Even though we hadn't chosen to include it in our adapted subject matter, this other information would come

to mind just the same. In fact, on the exam, we are often able to remember not only the information in the reduced (adapted) summary, but also what we had in our personal summaries that we chose to leave out of the reduced one. It is precisely because we waited to create our reduced summary that this information is still fresh in our minds.

So, let's get started, with a simple example of how the summary should be made, so you become familiar with the format.

The **FIRST SUMMARY** we are going to see has been done on the computer. It took about 40 minutes to write it out and the only thing left to do is to highlight the names of the divisions with the different colors, as well as write our pure fact associations in the right margin.

This deals with the existence of an imaginary planet. I have chosen this topic so that all of the information would be unfamiliar. Therefore, your own previous knowledge can't have any influence on the memorization process that will take place later on.

-PLANET TX-911075- (SUMMARY)

This planet has a diameter of 48,000 Km (about 30,000 miles—similar to Neptune), and is at a distance of 85 light years. They are 2500 years ahead of us.

Its inhabitants visited us on 3/4/1984. They are all 2 meters tall (about 6 feet). The women look like equilateral triangles with the vertex facing down. The men are longitudinal with enormous hands and heads. They are very peaceful and hard-working. The inhabitants are governed by a king (decorative role) who has 5 advisors (one per continent). They communicate by telepathy (other means of communication are prohibited because they create interference).

Given their great culture, education, and common ideology (there are no political parties) there is no need for laws, prisons, or courts.

HEALTH:

A) <u>Doctors</u> *(They wear colored bracelets on their right arm):*

- <u>Otorhinolaryngologist</u>: Green   - <u>Surgeon</u>: Yellow
- <u>Cardiologist</u>: Red

- <u>Massage Therapist</u>: White   - <u>Ophthalmologist</u>: Black

- <u>Orderly</u>: Brown   -<u>Nurse</u>: Blue

B) <u>Patients</u> *(A color-coded necklace indicates the severity of their illness)*
–<u>Slight</u>: Yellow   -<u>Less grave</u>: Blue   - <u>Very grave</u>: Gray

TRANSPORTATION: From urban transportation to traveling to their 4 satellites:
Preston, Galias, Rota, and Eulen (in order of proximity).

GEOGRAPHY: Its 4 continents are distributed as follows:

<u>-In the North</u> (Moderate climate): Copoal (Rich). Green Holm Oaks.

-In the Center (Warm): Ossen (Vast. 2 advisors). Acidic Oaks.
-In the South (Cold): Vitalia (Colder. Almost uninhabitable)
and Extradivarius ("poor"). Giant Pines.

TX has one saltwater ocean with no swell ("Tranquil-ity Lake"), since there is no wind, no seismic movement or faults, and it is less than 100 meters deep (approx. 300 feet).

*Their currency is called the Moderio. They come in de-nominations of 1, 10, and 100. Copoal also has 1000 Mode-rio coins.

The **SECOND SUMMARY** deals with a topic about the different possible circumstances when driving an all-terrain vehicle (4 x 4) in the forest. Carefully observe its:

- Design, taking up only 2/3 of the width of the paper.
- Title and key points highlighted in blue.
- Other subdivisions marked in red and green.
- An association made in blue ink in the right margin.
- Blue circles throughout the text of the summary, signaling the words related to the far-fetched associations written in the right margin.

Logically, the summary is reduced for our purposes, so that you can see the whole thing on one page.

These summaries are small because their source topic was that way. The point here is not to show a long or complicated summary, rather to help you understand how they are made.

If you compare the two summaries, the one done on the computer has **many advantages** over the handwritten one:

- It is much *clearer to read*.
- *We can fit more words* on one line (up to 10 or 12). With the handwritten ones, a lot less words

fit into the same amount of space, which has a negative effect on reading speed. This is due to the fact that our peripheral vision will always be the same; in both cases, we will get through one line of text in two photographic jumps. More words fit in a computer-made summary, and therefore, we take in more information with each jump.

- If you have a computer, try making your summaries with one of the *computer programs* on the market that write as you speak. They do make some mistakes, but this will also make you review them, which is another memoristic advantage. Even so, you can save a lot of time if the program is good and if it works well with your voice, which is not always the case. Try one. If you like it and it saves you time, keep using it. If not, then forget about it, and off you go.

I am trying to get the companies that make these programs to create a highly effective, low-cost program that I can provide for my students. Hopefully I will be able to do this soon, and you will have it available on my Website.

Making Mental Maps

The mental map for each topic should only take up **one side of a sheet of paper**. If the topic is small, we can fill it in with some extra information, as well as write in the far-fetched associations we have created to memorize the pure facts. However, don't overdo it because we already have all of the detailed information in our summary.

The mental map, most importantly, should be **pleasing to the eye** and comfortable to study, because its main mission is to provide us with a quick photographic representation of the skeleton of the topic.

Just like we did before, we are going to use **highlighters**, which will make it easier for us to move faster around the diagram without getting lost. We will use them in the same manner as we did with the summaries, meaning that each color will highlight the title in the topic that it corresponds to, according to the order we have stipulated earlier.

We will also use the **blue pen** to write the far-fetched associations that we want to reflect on the map. It is a good idea to write them after the same symbol you used on the summaries.

In order to make a mental map, which, as you know, will represent the true skeleton or structure of a topic, it is necessary to possess great knowledge of this topic. This is why it will always be **the last thing** that we prepare, after having created and understood the summary.

The title of the mental map, as well as the topic number (if there is one), should be placed in the center of the page and framed. We will then arrange its main components on branches, starting at the top (at 12 o'clock), and continuing **clockwise**.

The title of the topic (situated in the center of the map) and these main branches will be highlighted in blue.

We should only write individual words on our maps, or at most, **short phrases**, without going into depth or addressing difficulties we may have, so that they are easy and comfortable to read.

Mental maps will make it possible for us to achieve important photographic retention of its contents, and if necessary, it will also allow us to easily **add any new interesting facts** in the future.

Academic students (not competitive exam candidates) ideally should make the summaries of each topic **in class**, as they are taught and while the teacher is explaining them. Who better to clear up any doubts that may arise?

Mental maps, on the other hand, should be done later, **at home**, which is also a good way to review the topic.

Unlike traditional outlines, which are all similar due to their linear style, a mental map is more or less circular and unique to each topic. This circular shape together with the different colors will *make memorization considerably easy*, as well as help with review. This will directly affect how fast you then memorize the corresponding summary.

With our summaries and our mental maps, we will have completed our personal subject matter.

This **first mental map (page 134)** corresponds to a very simple topic which deals with driving a 4 x 4 all-terrain vehicle in the forest, whose summary you can see on 135.

Pay close attention to its:

- Circular design.
- Title and key points highlighted in blue.
- Other new divisions which, stemming from the main parts (or key points highlighted in blue), are marked in red.
- The new subdivisions, stemming from the afore-mentioned divisions in red, that are now highlighted in green.

The **second mental map** belongs to the summary written on the computer about an unknown planet.

Carefully observe its design and the correct use of the highlighters. (See page 133.)

This map, unlike the first, contains an enormous number of pure facts (although they are still not written on it).

We will have to memorize these facts using their corresponding far-fetched associations.

We will only memorize those associations that we have written on the mental map (with our blue pen). The rest of them will be memorized in the next summary, because that's where we will find them.

The mere act of looking at each mental map for a few seconds will already help us memorize it, thanks to the work that our photographic memory is doing automatically and unconsciously.

By using mental maps to study, it will be easy for us to retain the main idea of a topic, which is really most important at the beginning, and is the first thing we should do. We will also memorize the secondary ideas with the same ease.

2. Memorization

Although it may not seem like it at first, the actual memorization of the topic is the **shortest** part of the study process. As students gain more practice and ability, this will become even shorter.

Normally, after making a summary, students who have had enough practice and training **will, at the same time, have been able to memorize the topic at hand perfectly**. This occurs especially if the summary has a lot of pure facts ("the most difficult") and if they have been associated correctly (with far-fetched associations) after having finished the summary or while creating it. This last one: creating and writing the associations while you are writing your summary, as they come up, is something that I advise you to do as often as you can. Not only will this help you save time, but it will also help you relax your mind frequently, by means of the continuous escape to your fantasies, stopping your writing for a moment and imagining something fantastic for a few seconds.

Someone may still be asking, "Why on Earth do we make the mental maps, then?"

The answers are simple: In order to improve and accelerate the structural knowledge of each one of the topics.

For the global memorization process. After memorizing a mental map, you will have "little informer" in your head that facilitates the memorization of the corresponding summary because you will know very well what the main and secondary ideas are about. It's as if someone were saying to you, "Talk to me about this! Now talk about that!"

For the future and necessary reviewing that you will have to do. You will soon discover that they make an excellent tool for this task.

Memorizing Mental Maps

FIRST, we will memorize the **mental maps**, before the summaries. We should always start studying with the broadest and least profound structures, and then work our way up to the most complex and detailed information, which we will find in our summaries. In other words, we will go more in depth, little by little, as we acquire more and more knowledge on the topic.

Remember that we should first and foremost learn the structure of each topic: its main parts and divisions—in short, its skeleton. This is why we need to create these maps, which allow us to see the whole topic at a glance and at once. Later, the time will come to progressively memorize the most profound and complex facts that appear in the summary.

We shouldn't worry about investing time in studying the mental maps (really you can memorize a map in only one or two minutes). Make sure to give it a good photographic design.

IMPORTANT: THESE MENTAL MAPS, AS I AM DESCRIBING THEM, ARE VERY DIFFERENT FROM THE DRAWINGS, OUTLINES, OR EVEN OTHER MAPS THAT OTHER AUTHORS RECOMMEND. THE WAY THE LATTER ARE MADE (QUITE DIFFERENTLY FROM MINE), TOGETHER WITH THE DIFFERENT WAY YOU ARE SUPPOSED TO WORK WITH THEM, MAKE THEM ALTOGETHER INFERIOR AND NOT AS EFFECTIVE AS THE ONES YOU ARE LEARNING ABOUT HERE.

The **memorization unit**, or, the facts that we should memorize first on the mental maps, is made up of each of the titles that we have highlighted *in blue*, because they represent the broadest concepts. In other words, we will make sure that we can mentally repeat the main parts of the topic at hand, meaning, only the names of the titles, without going deeper into the information contained within them.

Then, we will focus on the first title of the topic highlighted in blue, and we will memorize the sections within it, highlighted in *red* (if there are any). As we did before, we will only memorize the titles highlighted with this color (without more detail).

Once we know the names of any and all of the sections highlighted in red, we will do the same with the subsections in *green*, contained within the red ones. As you can see, we always memorize from greater to smaller.

Then, we have to completely memorize the first one of the blue sections on our mental map, with all of its information. **Read it as many times as you need to** (a trained mind

will only have to do this a few times) while **repeating it to
yourself in a low voice**. First use your own words, and then,
little by little, use a more and more technical language.

Then, right after that, we should check to see that we
have memorized the structure of the mental map and that
we are able to understand it and reason it out.

We should also make sure that we have memorized all
of the pure fact associations on our map perfectly.

After we have memorized a map, which will only take us
a few minutes, it will then be ready for its next phase: review.

We should only begin to memorize the summaries
when we have made sure that we have all of the mental
maps perfectly memorized. **This is the general rule** that
you should follow for now, although in time, and as you
become more of an expert, you will have to change this.
But, this we will see later on, when we talk about how to
memorize the summaries.

Memorizing the Summaries

We have already said that first we have to memorize
the mental maps, which won't take too much effort and
will be quite simple for us. Once we know these maps well,
we will proceed to memorizing the summaries.

In order to memorize the **summaries**, we will read
them with our photographic reading technique (we should
already be doing this with everything we read) two or three
times in a row (or however many times you need). Take
your time, reasoning out what you are reading and stopping any time you don't understand something.

We will continue to do the same with all of the sections in which the titles are highlighted in *blue*, until we
get down the **main idea** of each of them. Remember that

we shouldn't try to memorize all of the details of the topic at first. Rather, the contrary: we will go deeper and deeper into the material with each review.

We should read the whole topic this way, trying to understand and reason out the text in each one of the blue sections, making far-fetched associations with all of the pure facts that we come across. We should be writing these down at the same time in the right margin of the paper. We still shouldn't have touched the parts of the topic highlighted in other colors (red and green), because these belong to more minute and complex parts.

Once we know the general idea of each part of the topic belonging to a blue title, we will begin to work, in the same way, with the information under the titles highlighted in red. We should follow the same memorization process as we did before, without yet going into the text included in the green section, because this part of the topic goes into even more depth.

Finally, after having memorized all of the main ideas in the red sections, we will proceed to do the same with the green sections.

We should make sure, after reading a section or sub-section a few times, that we have been able to capture its main idea (no matter what color its titles are). After these first readings we will mentally tell ourselves what their main idea is and, just like with the mental maps, we will do this more and more precisely, and make it more and more technical as we go.

Keep in mind that the *reading speed* will be inconsistent at first because we have to reason out some of the information as we are reading (although, this is really something we should do when we make the summary), stopping as needed to do this. In the readings after that, and once we understand the topic well, our reading speed will reach its maximum.

We should memorize **the pure facts in the summary** by means of our far-fetched associations, as we explained before. Remember that they should be written after their symbol, in the right margin that we have reserved for this purpose. Most likely, you have already done this when you created your summary (which is advisable) and before you made your mental maps. In this case, just make sure that you know them well.

Important:

I remind you that we should not try to memorize the whole summary in one session. At first, it will be enough to get an **expanded general idea** (the main idea + certain simple details), doing without the more complex parts for the moment. It is better to take these on when we have a good grip on the topic in general.

Just like we were able to know the general idea of a topic thanks to the mental maps, the expanded general idea includes all of the information that we will assimilate the first time we memorize the summary (which is really the memorization phase). This is complete when we are able to know and explain the main idea of each one of the sections up to the green ones (without going any further, if there are more subdivisions).

To make an analogy, this expanded general idea would be the equivalent of the knowledge and experiences that we enthusiastically tell our friends and family when we come back from a vacation.

When we have memorized the expanded general idea of a topic, we can consider the summary memorization phase as complete. We will then go on to the third and last phase: review.

Therefore, the act of memorizing and that of reviewing go hand in hand, and we can't separate them. We will really be talking about *memorization-review*. As I have said before and I now repeat, the following is of utmost importance:

We will be memorizing new facts and information in the successive reviews, in which at the same time we will also be consolidating what we have already memorized in the previous reviews.

This rule of memorizing in successive reviews is the best possible way to do so, *technically* (we memorize the most complex parts at the end, only after we have gathered enough knowledge to do so), and *psychologically*, because when we sit down for the first time to memorize the summary, we will feel very comfortable, without any psychological pressure, or any other pressure. This is because we don't expect ourselves to memorize the whole thing at once. Rather, only memorize the more superficial and simple information—that which we feel like memorizing because we consider it easier or more attractive, leaving the rest for future memorization-review.

When students have assimilated these memorization techniques well and they have enough experience with the material, it will be gratifying for them to see with their own eyes how they can even memorize the summaries (at least most of them) as fast as they make them. Therefore, when they finally get to making their mental map, they will already know the topic and be able to explain it correctly and in some detail.

The exception to this is when the students still don't have enough practice, in which case they should follow the general rule of memorizing the mental map first and then the summary, the exact opposite order in which they are made.

Little by little, and as you notice you are remembering the facts from each topic easier, you should change this initial strategy and start memorizing at the same time as you are making your summary. This way of working is incredibly efficient and will save you considerable amounts of time with practice, you will eventually start memorizing without even realizing it, unconsciously. This also means using less effort, saving energy, improved concentration, and psychological euphoria when you see how beneficial it is to study like this.   However, learning to study has its necessary stages, like everything in life, so lets focus again on the beginning and continue on.

Next, together we are going to memorize a topic in which the facts are completely unknown to you. It's much better like this because it allows us to see how effective our techniques really are.

When you finish and you really have a grasp on how to work with and memorize the example topic, I recommend that you get to work and practice these techniques with some other topic you have, so as to start becoming more agile and more confident.

I am going to ask that you please mind every detail as you begin, and don't rush. You must go carefully through every step. Deal?

Memorizing the Example Topic

As you know, in our study process we had to go through three phases:

1. Making the personal subject matter (summaries and mental maps).

2. Memorizing.

3. Reviewing.

The first thing that we need now is an initial topic (raw topic or base topic). So that no student has any advantage over another, the information in the topic we are going to memorize is completely fictitious. This topic is about a supposed civilization on another planet.

But first of all we are going to do a very important **first exercise**. Grab a pen, three or four sheets of paper, and a timer. Come on! I'll wait for you....

After reading this, copy the topic below with your pen, calmly and at a normal speed. Time how long it takes you to do this.

When faced with an essay exam, it is really important to know how fast we write. Keep in mind that you should have good handwriting and no spelling errors, and it should be easy to understand. Furthermore, you have to try to write out your exam with clear ideas. It should be enjoyable and easy-going, linking the facts together coherently and logically.

This topic will take up about four sheets, using one side, or *40 minutes of actually exposing it* at a normal writing speed. Because you will write faster than if you were actually taking the exam, you only have to copy it—you don't have to think—it will take you about 32 minutes (more or less) to finish copying it if your writing speed is average.

PLANET TX-911075

This is about a far off land, not visible from Earth, however, we have some knowledge about it, thanks to the information given to us by some extraterrestrial beings who descended on our planet on 3/4/1984.

They told us that their world is much more advanced than ours. There could be about 2,500 years difference between us.

The general organization is quite similar to ours in almost everything. This planet, found at a distance of 85 light years from us, is inhabited by some very peaceful and hardworking beings. According to what they told us, it looks a bit like our planet Neptune. It has the same equatorial diameter, 48,000 kilometers (about 30,000 miles), as our neighbor in our solar system.

Their healthcare system is also very advanced, just like the rest of the systems there.

The medical staff is distinguished by bracelets that they wear on their right arm, which identifies them and also differentiates them from the rest of the healthcare specialists by color.

Here is how it is organized:
- *The ophthalmologist wears a black bracelet.*
- *The cardiologist wears a red one.*
- *The otorhinolaryngologist, a green one.*
- *The surgeon, a white one.*
- *The massage therapist, a white one.*
- *The nurses, blue.*
- *The orderlies, brown, etc.*

The patients, on the other hand, wear a necklace that shows how serious their illness is, also color coded:
- *The very gravely sick wear a gray necklace.*
- *Those less grave wear a blue one.*
- *The slightly ill wear a yellow one.*

There is urban (within the same city), interurban, intercontinental (between the four continents that make up the planet), and space transportation. The latter travels to the four inhabited satellites of the planet. Their names are: Preston, Galias, Rota, and Eulen, named in order from the closest to the farthest.

Their trade system is also very sophisticated, although they do have currency which is called the Moderio. There are only denominations of one, ten, and one hundred, except on the richest continent, Copoal, which also has one thousand Moderio coins.

The rest of the continents are distinguished by other characteristics of their own. Vitalia, for example, is extremely cold, which makes it almost uninhabitable. Extradivarius is the poorest continent in comparison with the others, although poverty on this planet is relative. All of its inhabitants extraordinarily have all of their needs covered.

The inhabitants communicate through telepathy. Any other form of communication is prohibited since it could produce interference with other systems that exist on the planet.

Planet TX-911075 is governed by a king-like figure, who has five advisors, each of which carry out their tasks on a determined continent. Ossen, the largest continent, has two advisers given its immense size.

The climate can be divided into three concrete regions or zones. The coldest region is in the south, where Vitalia and Extradivarius are. The warmest part is in the center of the planet, where the continent Ossen is located. Lastly, the mildest area is in the north, where the last continent, Copoal, is located.

The vegetation is mainly composed of giant pines in the south, concretely in Extradivarius, an abundance of green holm oaks in the north, and in the central region of the planet there is a strange type of tree that grows, called acidic oak.

The rest of the planet, or that which unites and intertwines the continents together, is an enormous salt-water ocean. It is almost stagnant since there are no waves. This is due to the fact that there is no wind in the atmosphere, no seismic movement or faults and particularly because the ocean is not very deep in any given spot, less then one hundred meters (300 feet). It's not surprising that the ocean is commonly known as "Tranquility Lake."

It is interesting to note politically that there are no laws on "TX." They are unnecessary, given the high cultural level of the people and their exquisite education. This is why the king doesn't really play much more than a decorative role. All the people share the same ideology and therefore, there are no political parties. There aren't any prisons, courts or anything of that sort, either. All of these things belong to a distant time in the past, becoming part of history many hundreds of years ago.

Lastly, it is important to note that the average build of the inhabitants is exactly two meters tall (6 feet), for men and for women. The women have smaller heads and they are shaped more like equilateral triangles with the vertex pointing down. The men, on the other hand, have very longitudinal bodies and they don't have any other noticeable features except their heads and hands, which stand out for their disproportionately large size.

* * *

Good. By now you should know your writing speed, thanks to which you will now be able to take into consideration for the essay exams, when you are preparing your adapted summaries to the exposition time that you are given on the exam.

As you can see, I have pretty much respected the rule about using "new paragraphs" when changing ideas. Nevertheless, just like most of the "raw topics," it is quite unorganized, even though it doesn't seem like it at first. For example, it talks about the figure of the king, then the climate and then goes back to talk about politics. Also, the physical characteristics of the extraterrestrials aren't mentioned until the end of the topic (which seems like it's just an extra "blurb" at the end). This should be at the beginning, when our curiosity to know interesting things is peaked, especially with such graphic details.

Now, create your own summary of the topic. Give it a more logical order, which will definitely help with comprehension and later with your memorization speed. Clean it up and take away all of the fluff or filler you come by, because these don't provide you with any information. However, do respect all of the pure facts in the topic.

Keep the right margin clear so that you can later write all of your far-fetched associations in blue ink, and remember to use another pen, a black one, to write out the summary itself. Don't forget to highlight it later.

When you have finished, and **only** when you have finished, you can read on and compare yours with mine.

Although it is easy to understand, there are many pure facts contained within it. This is precisely where the difficulty lies for other students (not including you), because they don't know how to memorize them.

Did you make your summary already? Good; then, take a look at mine and, if you want, we can go ahead and memorize it together.

On the page in color you will find part of this summary highlighted, so that you can see how the highlighters are used here.

PLANET TX-911075
(Summary)

The planet is 48,000 kilometers (30,000 mi.) in diameter (similar to Neptune) and at a distance of 85 light years. They are 2,500 years ahead of us.

Its inhabitants visited us on 3/4/1984. They are all two meters tall (6 feet). The women look like equilateral triangles with the vertex downwards. The men are longitudinal with enormous hands and heads.

They are very peaceful and hardworking and they are governed by a king (decorative) who has five advisors (one per continent). They communicate through telepathy (other means are prohibited because they create interference).

Their great culture, education and common ideology (there are no political parties) makes the existence of laws, prisons and courts unnecessary.

HEALTH:

Doctors (They wear color-coded bracelets on their right arm):

- *Otorhinolaryngologist: Green*
- *Surgeon: Yellow*
- *Cardiologist: Red*
- *Ophthalmologist: Black*
- *Massage Therapist: White*
- *Orderly: Brown*
- *Nurse: Blue*
-

Patients (A necklace indicates how seriously ill)

- *Slight: Yellow*
- *Less grave: Blue*
- *Very grave: Gray*

TRANSPORTATION: From urban travel to going to their four satellites: Preston, Galias Rota and Eulen (in order of proximity).

GEOGRAPHY: Its four continents are distributed as so:

- In the North (Moderate climate): Copoal (Rich). Green Holm Oaks
- In the Center (Warm): Ossen (Vast. Two advisors). Acidic Oaks
- In the South (Cold): Vitalia (Colder. Almost uninhabitable) and Extradivarius ("poor"). Giant Pines.

TX has one saltwater ocean with no swell ("Tranquility Lake") because there is no wind, faults or seismic movement, and it is less than 100 meters deep (approx. 300 feet).

Their currency is the Moderio. There are denominations of 1, 10 and 100. Copoal also has 1000 Moderio coins.

Memorizing the Example Summary

Because this topic is full of pure facts, the far-fetched associations that we make will involve memorizing practically the whole topic.

The first thing that we have to do is *look at the title* carefully. Imagine for a moment that in your subject matter you had many more planets (in other different topics) and each one of them had its own particular characteristics.

Without any doubt at all, it would be an extremely unpleasant experience (which I'm sure has happened to the majority of students) if on an exam, they asked you a question about a certain topic, and you, knowing the answer perfectly, confuse its characteristics with those of another similar topic. Even though you knew both topics, you didn't know in this case if you were talking about planet "TX–911075" or planet "TV–811063," just to name another similar planet, for example. Hasn't this ever happened to you?

Of course, if there were no other planets in your subject matter, you couldn't get confused, but in this case, let's suppose that there are more planets and you have an important exam on astronomy and life on other planets.

I apparently want to complicate things for you a little bit here as you memorize this topic. I say apparently, because really, you will see that this is, as we say, "a piece of cake" to memorize, and that we will never be able to get confused with the facts from other planets that form part of the subject matter. I will teach you to do this the most effective and foolproof way possible. Oh! And enjoyable, too, of course. Let's reduce our margin of error in this case, if you like, to 0.0%.

If you are ready, we can start, then, having a good time and enjoying ourselves for a while. Have fun!

"TX" brings the word "taxi" to mind, and its identification number, "911075," could be transformed into the word "butterfly," for example. You remember how we transform numbers into letters, right?

9	1	1	0	7	5
B	T	T	R	F	L
P	D	D			
V					

With the letters placed in this position it is quite easy to find a word, or phrase that includes all of the letters that are going to substitute the planet's identification number.

You should choose only one of the possible letters from each vertical column. In this case, you can see the word "butterfly" right away. If you can't find a word, don't hesitate to use the dictionary to help you. In any case, you could always, as a worst-case scenario, use the mental chart to get by. You could link the words like this: "taxi–potato –rifle," "potato" and "rifle" being the words we get from our diagram.

How about a taxi driver who picks up a client, only to see that it is a talking Potato, who has turned violent and holds him up with a giant rifle.

Well, in this case, we'll stick with the words "taxi" and "butterfly."

Imagine a city, with its streets crowded with enormous "taxi-butterflies" that are flying low. The people raise their hand to call them and the "taxi-butterflies" go down toward the sidewalk. Without making them stop, the people who are calling the taxis hop on them.

Take a good look now. The words that substitute the title "taxi" and "butterfly" will work as wild cards to help us not to confuse the topics. Because these two words are exclusive to this topic, we will always know that we are referring to planet "TX–911075" and not a different one when we find one of these two words (taxi or butterfly) in a far-fetched association.

Now I would like you to visualize a really spectacular scene, only paying attention to the words in italics, without worrying about anything else:

The taxi driver has a cage-covered taxi with three wheels (triangular, like a "butterfly"). He has tons of gel in his "light hair" and is riding around the Nile River (as if he were in a taxi-motorboat). He speeds up, lifting the front wheel, popping it up on two wheels in order to "pass" other motorboats.

Observe:

- Tons of *gel* in the taxi driver's "light hair" will remind us of the fact that the planet is at a distance of "85 light years."
- A *cage*-covered taxi with *three wheels* is the translation of "48,000" kilometers, the diameter of the planet. 48 is "cage" in our chart, and the three zeros are the wheels. Remember that it was a triangular motorboat.
- In the *Nile* River on *two wheels*, is "2,500," the years that they are ahead of us. The number 25 is "Nile" in our chart and the two zeros equal the two wheels, which is how the motorboat ends up when the taxi driver speeds up, lifting the front wheel, to pass the other boats.

Furthermore, the topic says that "its inhabitants visited us on **3/4/1984.**" Logically, because this date is a pure fact, we have to translate it into another far-fetched association.

The best and most efficient way to translate a date is to always do the following:

- If the year is in the 20th century, only take the last two digits (for example, "84" from "1984").
- If the year belongs to the second millenium, 1001–2000, choose the last three digits (for example, "475" from "1475").

According to this system, the date the extraterrestrials visited us, 3/4/1984, would be reduced to "3484" and we would have to find a word that corresponds to this number. We really don't need our chart for dates because we don't have to put any information in order. Nevertheless, we are going to use it in this case, splitting the number in half, because I don't see any word that substitutes the number "3484."

We can get the word "make" and "juice." It doesn't matter if the words are from your chart or not. What matters is that, because these extraterrestrials are not only hard-working but also very peaceful, their leader told his assistant, as he saw us Earthlings for the first time:

"Make juice!" and they immediately took out some glasses of some beautiful, cold, red fruit juice for us, to show us that they come in peace.

Perhaps in the future, we may not know for sure that this date refers to the arrival of the beings from planet TX–911075, or if it refers to the arrival of other beings from another planet.

In order to avoid getting confused, we will include one of our wild cards in the far-fetched association: "taxi" or "butterfly," whichever you prefer. We could also use the "taxi driver" with the gelled-up hair, because we have already used him in the far-fetched association at the beginning of this topic, and of course has a lot more to do with "taxi." For example:

When everyone is about to drink the fruit juice, the taxi driver shows up. He is angry because he ran out of gel (you can imagine him shaking the bottle). He yanks someone's

juice out of their hands and, since it is sticky, tries to use it to slick his hair back, as if it were hair gel.

Now, do the section on "**health**" on your own. It is simple and you are now becoming an advanced student. In order to do this you will have to substitute the doctor's *specialty* and the corresponding bracelet *color* for something that they suggest to you. Then, create a far-fetched association with both things.

For example: an eye and an ear for the eye doctor and the otorhinolaryngologist (or the ear, nose, and throat doctor), respectively. You could visualize a police officer for the color blue and a polar bear for white, the two corresponding colors. Can you imagine him giving a massage with his huge paws? You should do the same with the *patients* and with their necklace colors.

Let's memorize the **four satellites** in order from the closest to the planet to the farthest. I want you to say and visualize the following sentence for this:

I am going presto (quickly) to Gallia (the Gaul, France) because the Eiffel Tower has spontaneously started to rotate. When I get there, I see all of the people eulogizing the tower as if it were a magical spiritual icon.

Notice how the words in italics effectively substitute the names of each of the satellites. The fact that the Eiffel Tower is rotating suggests France (Gallia) to me. But how will we know that these satellites belong to planet "TX–911075" and not to another one?

Well, it is simple. It just so happens that when we arrive to Paris, we see that the famous tower is not really rotating on its own, rather:

Our dear taxi driver is pulling it in circles with his taxi.

Next we can associate the **continents** as so:

Vitalia is the coldest. Therefore the people have to have more "vitality" in order to go from place to place and not get frozen along the way.

Imagine that the taxi drivers with slick hair are the ones who go fastest and have the most vitality, just to assure yourself that you are talking about planet "TX–911075" and not a different one.

Copoal is the richest planet. Its inhabitants' gold "cups" shine.

Again, so as not to get our planets confused, we could see the taxi drivers scooping out their hair gel from large golden cups.

Oh! I hope all you taxi drivers out there can forgive me! I salute you, and...ahem, thanks for your help!

Ossen is the most vast and extensive, and almost expresses this in its name: Ossen is like a "Dozen" times bigger.

Extradivarius is the poorest. Its inhabitants are so sad about being poor they all play sad songs on the violin, an "Ex-Stradivarius," a cheaper version of the authentic Stradivarius.

You can make other, slightly less effective associations by simply underlining or marking the initials of the different coincidences. You should always do this with a blue pen, so as not to get confused.

For example:

The Poorest continent has giant Pines.

A few more associations:

The men have large hands and heads because they are accustomed to carrying enormous glasses of fruit juice on their heads and in their hands when they go visit other planets. This way, they don't need trays (imagine them doing a balancing act).
The women have a triangular shape, just like a butterfly.

You can do the rest of the associations needed to complete the memorization of all of the pure facts yourself. You don't have to do it right now. You could do them another day, on a second memorizing-review.

Read the summary three or four times, using your photographic reading technique, but not too quickly. Use a pen as a pointer. Make and relive all of the associations we have made. Write them in the right margin with your blue pen (don't forget to put your symbol before the association). Because there will be a lot of them, if they don't fit in the margin of your summary, you can use the back of the sheet or use another one.

Then make the mental map for the topic.

In theory, we should make the mental map before memorizing the topic, but because the associations come quickly (do they not?) and this topic is **quite dense** (due to a high proportion of pure facts), you can do a lot of them before making the map.

I am going to ask you to try to remember it tomorrow. Try to recite it, and then try again after a week and see what happens.

The last step is to **REVIEW** the summary.

3. Review

The first reviews, called *initial reviews*, **overlap with the memorization phase**. This means that at the same time we review the already memorized facts that made up the expanded general idea of the topic (what we have just done with the topic of the planet), there comes a new memorization of the information, complementary to the expanded general idea. These are ones that we had left to memorize later and they are more and more in depth as we go.

I remind you that memorizing the mental map of a topic gives us its general idea, and the first time we memorize the summary we memorize the expanded general idea of this topic, so, logically, we memorize more information than is on the map.

With the successive reviews, what we are really doing is fulfilling a double objective:

- First reinforce all of the facts that we have already memorized, consolidating them in our memories, little by little.
- Memorize the topic a little bit deeper with each review, progressively incorporating the more complex or minute facts into our memory bank. These are the facts we did not include in the first memorization phase—that is, the ones we have to leave for later, when we have a much better grip on the topic.

This is why the correct way to refer to this phase in the study process is to call it the *review-memorization* phase, because both activities are done at the same time.

The review is a fundamental part of the study process that often isn't given the importance it deserves. It is common to underestimate it too much, resulting in poor retention of the "memorized" facts, which could mean memory failure at the time of the exam.

The review is what takes the longest, at least at the beginning, totaling about 90% of the total time dedicated to studying. Therefore, it is necessary to choose the right moment to review our subject matter. It will often be wise to take advantage of certain "lags" in the day, like the few minutes that we spend waiting in line, at the bus stop, during our recovery time between sets at the gym, and so on.

Next, we are going to see the different types of reviews that we have to carry out.

Initial Reviews

These are the first reviews that we have to do. After memorizing a mental map, we will review it mentally, without writing. The extra time that it would take to write would work against us, so we should say all of the information in it to ourselves.

Next we should make sure that all of the information that we have exposed in our review coincides with the contents on the mental map. If not, we will check to see where we have gone wrong and correct everything we need to. If we get stuck in these first reviews, its no problem, because we have the map (right in front of us) to use as support, as much as we need to keep ourselves from getting blocked.

These reviews **should be done daily**, twice with each mental map, leaving a few hours between both reviews. (It is best to do one in the morning and one in the evening or at night.)

The initial reviews won't take up much time, and should be done until we acquire good, solid knowledge of the topics and we have good command of the maps in such a way that we can go a while without reviewing them. The usual practice is to review two times per day, for a week, although some students may need more or less time to do this, depending on their technique, their ability, and the difficulty of the topic.

Also understand that doing these first reviews for a week is quite standard and, with practice, students will find that they have full control over the topics faster and faster, which translates into the review times becoming progressively shortened. A force within you will make you feel that you know the topics well and that you are reviewing in excess, wasting time as a result. This feeling is different for each student, so the decision to make depends on everyone's own criteria.

Due to their size, we will only dedicate one day to reviewing the *summaries.*

Remember that in the week of initial reviews there is an overlap, which, given its importance, I have spoken so much about before. This, as you know, consists of progressively memorizing the most in-depth and complex facts that we have left to memorize, together with reviewing what we have already memorized.

Eventually, we will end up with more and more maps and summaries to review, because we will continue getting more and more new material. These should be incorporated into the review phase as we go.

When we have a considerable number of topics in the review phase and we don't have enough time in the day for more, we should stop memorizing and dedicate ourselves exclusively to reviewing both the maps and the summaries, until they are all solidly reinforced in our memory. We can then say that we have completed the **first review phase**.

Notice how we give priority to reviewing over memorizing. It would be a shame if, for not having spent a little more time reviewing, the facts from the topics we have already memorized (and not reviewed enough) began to get "scattered" in our memories.

We then will begin the **second** memorization-review **phase**, until we have once again added enough new topics to then dedicate ourselves again to only reviewing.

We should not forget to *include the topics from the previous phases* in the reviews. They still need reviewing because, if not, we would end up forgetting them and we would have wasted our time.

We should proceed in this way with the whole subject matter.

Some students may think that these are too many reviews. Well then, know that they are **really necessary** and, thanks to the reviews, we will have full command over each one of our topics perfectly. On the other hand, you will soon see that the review will only take us a few minutes on each topic.

These are the *general rules for everyone*, and where every student who knows what he or she is doing, should start.

The **students who are most highly trained will need fewer reviews**, just like they will also need less time to read, memorize and understand their subject matter.

They, better than anyone, will know the most effective study rhythm, meaning the time they will take to make their personal subject matter, memorize it, and review it, as well as the right amount of time to invest on each work phase. They will achieve all of this much more effectively and professionally.

Conferential Reviews

After the initial reviews, we will continue reviewing the topics without the need to have the subject matter near us as a crutch. This will really indicate to us which one of the possible reviews we are in.

If we still need the subject matter by our side because we get stuck every once in a while, we are still doing the initial reviews, as seen before. If we can re-create the whole topic in our minds precisely enough, we are then in the conferential review stage.

In the conferential reviews we will tell ourselves the information from each topic **"like experts"** as if we were in an auditorium giving a speech or a conference on them—hence the name.

It is good to try to imagine and feel this "conference" in our minds. We have to try to live it as if it were really taking place.

Unlike the initial reviews, we no longer need to have our subject matter next to us to compare what we are "conferencing" with what we have in our summaries and mental maps, although it is a good idea to contrast it later on, at night if possible, to verify how exact our knowledge is.

In the conferential reviews we will no longer distinguish between summaries and mental maps. We will simply limit ourselves to exposing all of the information contained within the topic, although it is true that the photographic help we get from our mental maps could initially be a sort of script for us, to help organize us as we expose the information.

The conferential reviews can and should be done in situations of **forced mental inactivity** in the day, to save time—for example, in spare moments that we have while we are waiting in the line at the bank, at the supermarket, etc.

When you do it that way, you will immediately see that reviewing this way, apart from being enjoyable, will keep you from getting bored.

Remember that we can review the topics in any order we like.

With successive reviews we will have full command of the subject matter, so much that we won't need to compare it at night anymore. We will be sure to have memorized it correctly and that we have comprehended it completely. We will then find ourselves in the last phase: the final conferential reviews.

Final Conferential Reviews

As we get to this phase only the students can decide how often they will review in the future. In principle, the moment has come to stop reviewing, until you finish with the whole subject matter, or at least for enough time to focus mainly on the other topics you have left to finish.

When reviewing the summaries and the mental maps **we should never write**. This is because that would be a waste of time. Those who get used to writing as they review should stop this bad habit because it is detrimental to their efficacy when they study. If on a personal level you think that you need to write because you lack mental concentration, you will improve your concentration day by day and with little effort, thanks to this active, fun, and totally efficient study system.

It is only advisable to write at the end, if we have to take essay exams. The best moment to do this is when we master all of the topics and we have to adapt our personal subject matter to the time allotted on the exam. This way we will build up resistance and fluency in our writing.

Reading-Reviews

This is the last type of review, which we can include whenever we want.

This review is good to do quite often at the beginning and above all with the summaries. In reality, with the mental maps, it's not really necessary.

It is also most appropriate, and really the only option, when there are only two or three days left before a competitive exam that you have been preparing for for a long time.

We can also review this way any day that we are too tired to make any other type of mental effort. However, be careful with too many bad days!

Some Final Advice

When you get stuck on a topic, you should think that it is almost always due to **lack of understanding**. This problem should have been solved at the beginning, when we made the summaries.

We have to be sure to master the subject matter **like experts** in the end, so that, no matter how twisted the questions can get on the exams, especially multiple choice tests, they will never catch us off guard.

With a little bit of **mental training** we can move around the subject matter quickly, clearly, and comfortably.

I must insist to those taking competitive exams that it is a very good idea to **expand on their subject matter** using other means such as the library, looking in encyclopedias, or in different books, watching films related to the topic (interesting, isn't it?), documentaries, etc.

In order to do this, and in the case of using books (which is the most common), it is enough to read the chosen information two or three times before you add it to the subject matter. It is good to take three or four days to expand on the subject matter, when you have mastered the final conferential reviews and close to exam time. This way, you will be able to remember it easily, without having to review it.

Finally, in the last two or three days before the exam (depending on how long our subject matter is) the reviews will become **exclusively reading reviews,** and, if possible, relaxed reading. They are the most appropriate because, among other things, they are the quickest and require the least amount of mental effort, which will help us get to the exam more rested and with a certain "urge" to transmit all of the information that we have memorized.

First all of the maps should be reviewed, then all of the summaries. If we have time, we will review the whole subject matter twice. However, if it were especially large or our reading speed weren't supersonic yet, we will only review it once.

When we are already working on the final reviews, we will not only feel like experts; we will feel **calm and relaxed**. We shouldn't think too much about the exam because the die is pretty much cast.

Competitive exam candidates will have to be careful to unite **each and every one of the requisites** they are asked for in their exam session, such as the right documentation, certificates, etc.

Likewise, all of the candidates who have to take a medical exam should be very careful with whatever they ingest that day, solid or liquid, and the days before this exam, to avoid raising their blood-sugar level, cholesterol, blood pressure, etc. They should be especially careful **NOT TO TAKE ANY MEDICINE,** no matter how much the rules state that all they need is a doctor's note to verify this, or that it only has to be communicated to the medical board.

None of this. Unfortunately, I have seen too many cases of *unfair elimination of aspiring candidates* from a competitive exam because they were taking prescription medicine for a flu, a cold, or a cough.

For the time being they are declared "unsuitable," only then to be disqualified for this, even though they had informed the medical board of their situation, who, more often than not, simply limit themselves to certifying any proof they find in the analyses, and then just wash their hands of the matter. The slowness and clumsiness of the subsequent bureaucracy is often the last straw that brings down the trusting candidate, who hadn't been precautionary enough and trusted in that a bureaucratic legality could get them out of this sticky situation.

On the day of the exam we should only think about **being relaxed and having a good day,** so that our knowledge flows through us naturally and avoids any psychological tricks. *We must not review anything!* The only thing we would achieve with this would be to get more anxious, and we could fool ourselves into thinking that we have doubts in the last minute, making us insecure or even raising our nervous tension, which, as you know, is not at all beneficial.

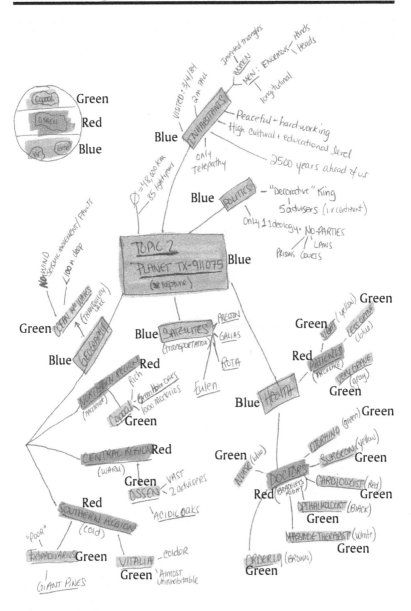

Green
Red
Blue

INHABITANTS?
Blue
VISITED: 3/4/84
2 m TALL
Inverted triangles
WOMEN
MEN : EYEBROWS / HANDS / HEADS
longitudinal
Peaceful + hard-working
High cultural + educational level
2500 years ahead of us
only telepathy

Ø = 48,000 km
85 lightyears

POLITICS
Blue
"Decorative" King
5 advisers (1 x continent)
Only 1 ideology • NO-PARTIES
LAWS
PRISONS COURTS

NO WIND
Seismic movement / faults
1,100 m. deep

TOPIC 2
PLANET TX-911075
(≈ Neptune)
Blue

OCEANS AND WAVES
(TRANQUILITY LAKE)
Green

GEOGRAPHY
Blue

SATELLITES
(TRANSPORTATION)
Blue
PRESTON
GALIAS
ROTA
Eulen

NORTHERN REGION
(moderate)
Rich
Red
Cocoa - Green hornoaks
1000 microbios
Green

CENTRAL REGION
(WARU)
Red

OSSEN
VAST
2 advisers
ACIDIC OAKS
Green

SOUTHERN REGION
(COLD)
Red

EXTRADIVARIUS
GIANT PINES
Green

VITALIA
- colder
Almost uninhabitable
Green

HEALTH
Blue

SIGHT (yellow)
LESS GREAT (blue)
Green

PATIENTS
(TRICELUXE)
Red
VERY GRAVE (gray)
Green

DOCTORS
Red (BRACELETS RIGHT)
ALLIANCE (blue)
Green
OTORHINO (green) Green
SURGEON (yellow) Green
CARDIOLOGIST (Red) Green
OPTHALMOLOGIST (BLACK)
Green
MASSAGE THERAPIST (White)
Green
ORDERLY (BROWN)
Green

Mental Map #1

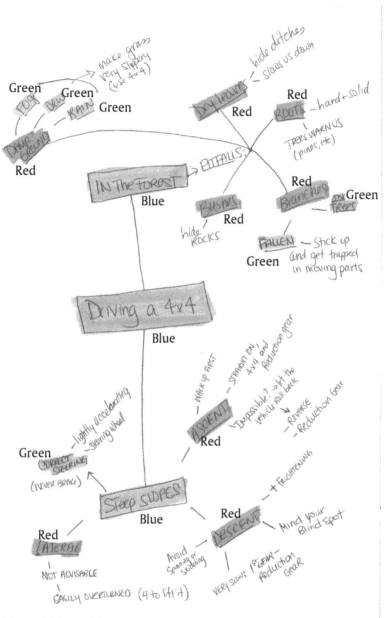

Green FOG   Green   make grass
        DEEP   RAIN   very slippery
               Green   (use 4x4)

DAMP GROUND
Red

IN THE FOREST
Blue

Driving a 4x4
Blue

Dry leaves — hide ditches
                — slows us down
Red

Red
ROOTS — hard + solid
            TREES WARN US
            (pines, etc)

PITFALLS?

Bushes
Red
hide ROCKS

Branches   Green
Red   IN TREES

FALLEN — stick up
Green   and get trapped
         in moving parts

WALK UP FIRST
ASCENT — STRAIGHT ON,
Red   4x4 and Reduction gear
         IMPOSSIBLE? → let the
            vehicle roll back
            — REVERSE
            — Reduction gear

Green   — lightly accelerating
DIRECT STEERING   steering wheel
(NEVER BRAKE)

Steep SLOPES
Blue

Red
LATERAL
NOT ADVISABLE
EASILY OVERTURNED (4 to lift it)

Avoid
Spinning or
skidding

DESCENT   — + FRIGHTENING
Red   Mind your
            Blind Spot
VERY SLOW: 1ST GEAR —
            Reduction GEAR

Mental Map #2

Blue Driving a 4×4 (summary)

Blue (A) IN THE FOREST

Pitfalls:

Red – DRY LEAVES : Hide ditches. Slow us down

Red – ROOTS : They are very hard and are solidly grounded. The trees (mainly pines and other resinous trees) serve as a warning of their presence along side the road.

Red – TREE BRANCHES : Appear suddenly, high or low.

Red – Fallen Branches : They can obstruct the underside of the truck and get trapped in the moving parts: the transmission, wheels, the brakes, etc.

Red – Bushes : They can hide rocks.

Red – Damp Ground :

   Green – FOG ⎫→ make the grass slippery.

   Green – DEW ⎬

   Green – RAIN ⎭→ use 4-wheel drive.

                                      * The ground is damp because the Frogs do a Rain dance.

Blue (B) STEEP SLOPES

Red · – Ascent : After going up on foot and checking the consistency of the ground, go, straight on, in 4-wheel drive using the reduction gear.

Red – Descent : More frightening. Mind your blind spot. Start manoeuvring slowly, trying not to let the vehicle spin or skid. Use the reduction gear in 1st.

Red – LATERAL : Should be avoided because the vehicle can be easily overturned, due to its high center of gravity. If it does turn over, it takes 4 people to lift it back.

   * control your steering using the wheel and light acceleration. Do not use the brakes.

CHAPTER 5

ACADEMIC AND COMPETITIVE EXAMS

Sooner or later the time will come for us to show off what we have learned, what we have memorized. The time has come to compete, to show what we know, and to know that we know what we know!

Here, our psychology and our emotional control will play a key role. Having good solid knowledge on any given subject is of no use to a student if he or she is unable to demonstrate it.

We are going to take a very close, professional look at all different types of exams in order to know each of them inside and out. I will show you the secrets held within each one of them.

We can initially classify the exams, academic exams, competitive exams, entrance exams, civil service exams, or any other type, into the following categories:

- Essay and short answer exams.
- Multiple choice tests.
- Oral exams.
- Practicals.
- Aptitude tests.

Besides physical tests and medical check-ups, which some may have to pass as part of some entrance or civil service exams.

Each type of exam has its advantages and disadvantages. Not all are to be prepared in the same manner. You shouldn't study the same way to pass a school exam, as you would for a competitive exam.

Essay and Short-Answer Exams

These exams can either be based on long-answer questions with quite a bit of time to answer, or on short-answer questions with less time to answer.

In the latter we should stick to the questions asked, avoiding wordiness or being long-winded. If they wanted us to write down more information, they would have given us an exam with long-answer questions and more time to develop an answer.

On essay exams you will have to do the following:

Read, and reread if necessary, the questions and instructions on the exam **thoroughly and calmly**. This is a good habit to get into, in order to avoid misinterpretations or misunderstandings.

At first, you have to take one or two minutes to **organize** the order in which you will answer the questions on the exam. The questions that are worth the most points and the ones we can answer best should take precedence.

It's a good idea to save the last five or 10 minutes for a **final review** if time allows.

It is much better to **write a little on each question** rather than to brilliantly respond to half of them, leaving the rest blank and unanswered. Many students think that if a competitive exam consists of four questions and they answer two of them perfectly, that they can get a sure 50% as their final grade. It really isn't like that. In general, you have to answer all of them, and well at that, in order to get a passing grade on the exam, regardless of whether or not it is enough to get a job.

A **brief statement** is always preferable. It should be clear and precise, and should specifically address the question at hand. It should not be verbose, poorly defined, poorly structured, or confusing.

Keep in mind that whenever we **want to write a lot** and quickly, we are more likely to get nervous and forget information, "stick our foot in our mouths," make mistakes, or commit spelling errors.

Use a lot of **full stops** because psychologically they give the favorable impression of both amplitude and brevity at the same time. Furthermore, the examiner will appreciate how clear and easy it is to read and correct our exam, which will give a better impression of us and reflect on our final grade. This tends to unconsciously raise our grade. Wouldn't the same thing happen to you if you were grading the exams?

Remember that **poor expression**, illegible or clumsy handwriting, spelling errors, and wordiness are penalized.

In the end, it might be interesting to summarize the question briefly, **using terminology and expressions from it**. This demonstrates that we haven't gotten off the subject and makes our answer seem more organized and convincing to the examiner. I advise doing this especially when we don't have enough information to answer the question well, in which case it would also provide us with a little bit of filler.

You should train by writing summaries of the subject matter **very quickly** in order to keep your hand from suffering premature exhaustion in the exam. Plus it helps to avoid bothersome writer's cramp.

If the exam has a mix of multiple choice questions and essay questions, we should make a sort of "**sandwich**" by answering the multiple choice questions halfway through the exam—the "bread" being the essay questions, which we will answer at the beginning and at the end of the exam. This will give our minds and our hands a break halfway through the test, and help us to still have energy by the time we get to the end of it.

Multiple Choice Tests

The first secret we need to know in order to take these exams lies in knowing that, unlike on essay exams, **you shouldn't memorize** anything from beginning to end. Not texts, and much less a whole subject matter. Only pure facts. Nor is it necessary to know how to explain or discuss anything.

On these exams, the student's **general educational and cultural level** is an important factor that must be taken into consideration. This is what allows the student to find the right answers, thanks to any and all previously acquired knowledge.

It is absolutely fundamental to **understand and reason out the subject matter** when we are studying it, because in these exams we will find a lot of twisted or even poorly founded questions. However, we can find solutions to these questions by understanding what they mean.

It is also of utmost importance to **read all of the questions carefully** and as many times as we need. The latter is very important, especially for those who really know their subject matter and, as they start reading a question, speed up and assume what is being asked. Many times, due to overconfidence, they fall for the "trick" in the trick question. After these exams, sometimes we hear unfortunate cries of regret like "How could I have gotten that one wrong?" or "I knew that one!" or "Ugh! What a stupid mistake!"

Be careful here because haste can often lead to confusion.

Sometimes when we read the question for the second or third time, we understand it better and find it easier to answer, just the opposite of what we had perceived the first time we had read it. This usually happens with questions that are **worded differently** from how we had studied the material, and also those that we didn't get, out of lack of attention or comprehension. This is why I must insist again on how understanding and reasoning the material are essential for passing these types of tests.

How Should We Answer Multiple Choice Tests?

Of course, we will begin with the first question, and then in order, we will calmly answer **all of the questions that we know for sure.**

After the first round, we shall **reflect on the following:**

Have we answered enough questions correctly to pass the exam?

Note! In this case, we are talking about pass/fail situations. I'm not talking about competitive exams in which barely passing doesn't cut it; rather it is necessary to get the highest grade possible.

A) *If the answer is yes* and we have time, we should first go back over the questions we have already answered in the first round, because those are the ones we know best. Also, this won't take long and is quite easy to do.

This way we will very conveniently check and make sure that we haven't made any "stupid" mistakes without realizing it.

If everything is correct, we will then carefully reread the questions that we haven't yet answered. We do this to check if there are any questions that we missed or that we can now answer either because the answer has come to us, or because the other questions we have answered have given us the necessary information to do so.

Logically, you would only do this when the wrong answers (called negative answers) count against you. If this weren't the case, you would have to answer all of the questions. The answers we aren't sure about should not be answered erratically. Rather we should try to use our intuition to answer them (look further along in "using your intuition to answer").

B) *If the answer is no, and we haven't answered enough questions* on the exam to get a passing grade, we will have to risk it. To do so, we must take the following mathematical formula into account:

"1/(the number of possible options - 1)"

Let's suppose, for example, that the exam has four possible answers (a, b, c, and d).

If we apply this simple mathematical formula, the result is: 1/(4-1) = **1/3**

The number "4" is the number of possible options.

This obtained value: "**1/3**," or if you prefer "**0.33**," **represents the mathematical balance or equality.**

Pay close attention! We can and should always risk losing 0.33 points or less for each negative answer (wrong answer) that we give. If they take away more than 0.33 points for each negative answer, then we should leave it blank.

Now, let's look at the denominator of the resulting fraction: 1/3. You can also interpret this fraction as: "For every three negative answers (the denominator) they take away one positive answer (the numerator "1"; this will always be 1)."

Imagine if, instead of telling us that for every *three* negative answers we lose one good (or positive) answer, whose resulting fraction, as we know, is 1/3, the results said that we would lose the point for a number of negative answers **greater than the denominator** of that fraction. For example, they could say that for every *four* negative answers we would lose one positive one, or even a number greater than 4. In this case, **we would undoubtedly risk all of them**, because mathematical probability would play to our favor, and in advantageous proportions.

I repeat: In this case, we should not leave any answer blank, but also, as I said before, you shouldn't answer erratically, rather use your intuition to answer the questions, as we will see ahead.

Notice how, in this case, in order for us to "risk it" clearly and with full advantage, the resulting denominator, being the number of errors needed to take away one point, would have to be greater than 3. What could also happen, although not often, is that the denominator could be less than 3 and, therefore, closer to 1. For example, if they said that for every two negative answers we lose one positive one, the resulting fraction would be 1/2. If this were the case, we should, in principle, leave the doubtful questions blank.

Nevertheless, among the doubtful questions that we leave unanswered, there are almost always some that we can narrow down to two or three of the given choices using process of elimination. In fact, there are very few times that we really have no clue as to what the answer may be because the question almost always "rings a bell" and we can usually eliminate one or more of the possible options. So, as we reflect on the doubtful questions we often say, "I'm sure that this is not the answer."

Once again, in these cases, we will also take the results of the formula into consideration when we answer them. After eliminating the answers that we are sure are wrong, there will be many questions that we have narrowed down to only two options (others down to three, etc.). So, our formula will change according to the doubtful options that remain. Therefore, we will end up using two or three different fractions for each group of doubtful questions on the exam. We should group them by the number of options that we have narrowed them down to. Logically, it is not the same to risk answering when you are doubting between four possible options than when you are doubting between two.

If our formula results coincide with the number of points we lose for each wrong answer, and we find ourselves in a state of mathematical equilibrium (in other words, it is exactly the same) answering this group of doubtful questions will also depend on our situation in the exam.

This state of mathematical equilibrium is quite frequent and, because it is a bit more difficult to calculate, we are going to look at it later on. You will understand it better when we evaluate this particular case in competitive or civil service exams, although if you want to know, when faced with mathematical equality, I would always risk it, but I would do it by trying to use my intuition to answer the questions, as we will see next.

Also remember that many times the best way to answer the questions, especially the doubtful ones, is by process of elimination.

Something very interesting that will happen to us more often than we would expect is that some of the exam questions and, more specifically, the way they are worded (although sometimes, and to a lesser degree, some of their answer options) can clear up doubts that we had on an earlier question, that we couldn't answer the first time around. So, keep this in mind.

Using Your Intuition to Answer

When the outcome of our aforementioned formula gives us a favorable mathematical probability, indicating that we should risk answering the questions that we have left blank (either because they were doubtful or we had no idea what the answer might be), we should *use our intuition to answer* the questions and mark one of them. We shall do this without any fear whatsoever, because we have nothing to lose.

The way to do this is the following:

The first rule to take into account when answering the doubtful questions with your intuition is that, most of the time, *the correct option is usually the first one that came to mind*. However, it is also true that, when we are reviewing our choices, if we are convinced that we have made a mistake, we should change it and mark the new answer that we think is correct.

In other words: if, after reviewing a question, another option clearly comes to mind, *we should choose this other option*, because statistics show that these changes are often correct.

If our formula indicates that we should risk answering the doubtful questions but we don't know which option to choose, *then it is best to assume there will be equality* in the final recount of the chosen options, when we add up and classify the options we chose (a, b, c, d, etc.) according to the number of times each letter comes up (which, as I demonstrate in my presential courses, happens quite frequently).

This is easy to demonstrate. For example, if any given person writes the letters a, b, c, and d quickly and arbitrarily, one below the other, and then counts them, they will see how, most often, the number of times that each letter appears is incredibly similar or the same.

This is why we should answer the questions we doubt by choosing the options (letters) that have come up least, and in the case of a "tie" or a close game, we should mark the letter that has not come up in the longest amount of time. This is because when the exams are made, those who create them almost always have a tendency of unconsciously compensating to even out the number of times each letter represents the correct answer.

In any case, don't get scared, and remember that we are starting with a favorable mathematical probability. That's why you have to "risk" the doubtful questions.

Further on, in the section on preparing competitive exams or entrance exams, you will find more information on all of this.

Oral Exams

We have to prepare these exams **as if they were essay tests.**

Having a **video camera** at home to record ourselves while we discuss a topic or when we are reviewing could be of immeasurable help for practicing.

While we are discussing a topic, we should **pronounce correctly** and, most importantly, we should speak slowly and not too loudly, because this could create added nervous tension.

Speaking slowly will help buy us time to better remember the facts that we have stored in our memory. It will also make it possible for us to enter into a higher state of relaxation, physically and mentally, which will be easier to achieve if we do not raise our voice too much.

Remember: It is better to **speak as slowly and quietly** as possible. We can analyze ourselves and see our progress with the video recorder.

If you are not very graceful, it is better to avoid making **gestures and unnecessary movements** with our body. In this case it is better to move slowly and only in precise moments, although it is true that using your hands to gesticulate can help some people.

When we get up from our seat to speak in the exam, we should walk slowly and calmly. You should employ the necessary techniques to control your nerves before you even get up from the seat and much before you start (sometimes more time is needed to do this, depending on the person). The whole idea is to avoid, at all times, any nervousness that can make us lose control.

You will find more information on this in the chapter on "control and relaxation techniques."

Use **sophrology** techniques. One of the most effective ones involves visualizing ourselves as if we were expert scientists who are giving a conference. The students who are listening are our audience, and the evaluator or evaluators are the journalists.

Visualize at night, in bed, which is when we are in a more receptive state for influencing our subconscious with these thoughts and sensations. Feel the classroom; smell it. You should try to feel comfortable and relaxed. You should also feel important. After all, you are the best scientist and expert in the material that you are discussing.

The day of the exam, you have to "self-hypnotize" and feel what you have been visualizing at night, as well as paying attention to the rest of the relaxation techniques if necessary. If they're not necessary, then all the better.

Competitive Exams

When we talk about competitive exams, we are referring to all types of exams that are based on exactly that: a competition. This includes international competitive exams for overseas jobs, entrance exams, civil service exams, state exams, and the like. On these exams, the one who "wins" or the one who gets one of the first positions and gets a job, always has a higher score than the one who simply participates.

It has often been said that "It's not whether you win or lose, it's how you play the game." Ha! Maybe in a children's or *amateur* track race, but not in an Olympic final, where the most important thing is to win (or at least that's what it looks like, given the evolution of today's competitive society).

In reality, the aforementioned phrase is in quotes because it is more of a consolation than anything else. Let's not be fooled. In an Olympic track and field final, just like on a state exam, the only one who really triumphs is the one who wins (at least they triumph more than the others as far as the audience, the press, and the media are concerned, right?). In our case it is the same. The ones who are able to pass their exam and get a position, triumph more. Therefore, this should be our highest goal: to pass the exam and get a position.

On an ordinary exam, given throughout the course of the school year, the whole class can pass, not a limited number of students. However, on a competitive exam, civil service exam, or the like, in which there are only 10 positions offered, it wouldn't make any practical difference to end up in 15th place or in 80th place. Passing in one of the top-10 positions is the only thing that matters. If we aren't lucky enough to have someone on the "inside" pulling strings for us, then we had better prepare the exam with professionalism, yet without forgetting to enjoy ourselves in the process. This way the preparation will be more enjoyable and we will get better results, even though it might seem hard to believe that both of these concepts are compatible.

Personally, I have always preferred competitive exams over school exams, because the former allow you more freedom to organize your time better; even though these exams are a bit more like a final exam in that they are extremely important and have such a high risk factor. However, it is true that many people, after passing these exams, keep on studying and preparing new exams in order to move up to a higher position at work or to change jobs.

The main advantage that a competitive exam has over an ordinary one is that we can organize our study time as we wish, without feeling pressured. If we don't feel like studying one day, there's no problem. We can even take some vacation time in the preparatory phase. As a general rule, we set our own work rate.

On the other hand, school or university students have to follow a strict and disproportionate syllabus, with too much material and a lot of "filler," which can often make one feel overwhelmed. In this case, the academic system forces students to work at a rate that is not their own.

Academic syllabi should really be more concentrated and more precise. They should include less material, getting rid of that which is outdated and useless (which, by the way, is so commonly included because of the interests of others, as usual). This way, they could also be much more profound, yet at the same time it would be much easier to follow them. This would also help achieve better future specialization.

I do indeed believe that neither you nor I can do anything about this, at least not for now. The best is to prepare ourselves for this exciting adventure of competitive exams! Are you ready? Okay then, let's continue on our journey.

Competitive Exams: Written Tests

This type of test is forms part of practically 100 percent of these exams. Some even have more than one written part. These tests can either be essays or multiple choice.

A) On the essay tests we should prepare an *adapted version of the subjects covered on the exam*, whose length coincides with the time that we have for expounding each one. These reduced topics are precisely those that will be on the exam.

This means that if we are given one hour to discuss each subject on our exam, it would be ridiculous for us to insist on memorizing 20 pages of a subject, which, even if we had memorized, would take us four or five hours to write out. This is logical, right? Well, you would be surprised at the number of students that have come to me, who had this very problem. This not only made them lose tons of time, but, furthermore, jeopardized all of the information that they had memorized due to having so futilely overexerted themselves.

Remember that the objective when these exams are in essay format is to *learn only what is necessary* to pass the exam, yet with as much reliability as possible. We will learn more about these things when we actually get the job and with practice, which is the best way to do so, anyway.

Also remember what we said about adapting the particular subjects to the time given for each one on the exam. These should be prepared close to the exam date and after having made sure that the structure of the exam hasn't been modified.

We also said, and just to review, that we should only include the most important information of all of the material contained within the given subject or topic, completing it with the information that we like most or with that which we know best. Likewise, we would have to exclude the material that, due to its nature or our own, is more difficult to memorize or remember.

B) On multiple choice tests, unlike essays, *the more extensive our subject is, the better.* We have already discussed this a few pages back, but I want to stress that on competitive tests it may even be necessary to expand on the subject at hand, with new information on topics that are similar to or that border it. These can be found in other books or notes, in libraries, on documentaries, etc. Later on the exam, quite frequently there are questions called "off the subject" questions, and sometimes nobody really even knows were they are taken from. Thanks to having extended our studies, there is a greater probability of answering these questions correctly, which is quite interesting because, in fact, answering these strange questions correctly usually earns the points that make the difference between those who get a position and those who don't, regardless of whether or not the latter are also "well-prepared."

As I have said before, and I cannot stress how important it is, it is fundamental to be able to *understand and reason out the topic or subject* when we are studying it. Understanding it correctly together with the appropriate association of all of the pure facts we find within it, should be more than enough to help us get 10 out of 10 on the exam.

It is also interesting to note that statistically, on multiple choice tests (which are more and more popular), those with a background in science often obtain better results than those who have studied arts and letters. This is just the opposite of what tends to happen on essay exams. This concept can help us choose a determined exam in the case that it takes place in more than one place at a time and the exams are of both types. But be careful! This is not meant to stop anyone or frighten anyone, much less someone who reads this book and uses the techniques and knowledge contained within it.

Competitive Exams: Answering Multiple Choice Tests

Of course, and just like we said about the multiple choice tests on general exams, on competitive exams we will also begin with the first question and continue on in order, answering the rest of them. After the first round, and supposing that the exam we are taking is the last part of the series of tests usually included in competitive exams, we shall take a moment to **contemplate the following:**

This is the last score to calculate into our final score. We will probably know what place we are in so far on the exam classification list (as well as the grade we have achieved so far and that of any other contestant that we want to check on). **If at this point, we are listed in one of the qualifying positions**—that is to say, among those who are passing—we maybe shouldn't risk answering any more questions. It all depends on the number of points that we have over the competitor who is the first one, just under the last qualifying place on the list. In other words, if there are 10 positions offered, the one who is in 11th place.

Let me give you an example, so that you can under-stand perfectly what I want to say.

Let's imagine a competitive exam which offers 10 job positions. Suppose that we are doing well, and we are in third place on the list.

No matter how many candidates are taking the exam, we should only be concerned with the points that the candidate in 11th place has earned.

We will know the difference between our points and number 11's points (because we should have checked the lists before going into the last exam), and we will also know how many points this last test is worth, because this should be previously stipulated in the exam rules and guidelines. If this were not the case, we should ask a member of the panel of judges or the committee for this information.

Then, by means of a simple mathematical calculation, we will add our previously accumulated score to the points we can estimate getting on this last exam. We get the lat-ter number from the number of questions on this last test that we believe we have answered correctly in our first round of answering.

On the other hand, and in the same way, we will add the points that the 11th candidate has so far, to the maxi-mum possible points they can get on this last test, this be-ing the improbable case of a perfect score.

If poor candidate 11th has no mathematical chance of equaling our score, we can definitely smile and relax. We would only have to check that we have correctly written our name and other information that is required of us. We could review what we have already answered, to be sure that all is correct and that we haven't made any care-less mistakes. If we have more time after this review, we can also review the rest of the questions, in case we have skipped over one that we can answer for sure.

But be careful: The second time around, only answer the questions whose answers we are 100% sure about! Only answer those that we skipped over before, but now can clearly see (sometimes this does happen). When faced with any doubts whatsoever, it is better not to answer. Why should we risk something that is already in the bag?

This, of course, is all under the assumption that the negative answers take points away from us, as is normally the case. If this were not the case we would have to answer all of the questions, but the ones we don't know should not be answered erratically. Rather we should use our intuition to answer them, just as we did with the general multiple choice exams.

On the contrary:

If candidate 11 can catch up to us, or if we are in 11th place (or in an even worse place) we will take this last part of the exam with the intention of getting the best score possible. In order to do this we will have to, once again, consider the mathematical formula we have seen before:

"1/(the number of possible options–1)"

Remember that we had said that on an exam that has four options (a, b, c, and d) this formula gave us a result of: "1/(4–1) = 1/3" and the value "1/3" or "0.33" represented the mathematical balance. We could and should always risk losing 0.33 points (or less) for every negative answer. On the other hand, if every negative answer takes away more than 0.33 points, then we should leave it blank.

Likewise, we also said that, if the denominator of the formula were to come up closer to 1—that is, if it were any number less than 3—the doubtful questions should initially be left unanswered because mathematical probability would work against us in this case.

However, if instead of three negative answers for every positive one, the number were greater than three (four or more) we should risk all of them, because we would have mathematical probability on our side. We shouldn't leave any question unanswered, yet, as we have said before, we shouldn't answer with no rhyme or reason. Rather we should use our intuition to answer the questions.

Multiple Choice Test Formats

Multiple choice exams can be classified into two different types:

A) THE CIRCLE THE ANSWER type. Many of these questions can appear in study guides geared toward the subject at hand, with practice questions and answer keys, such as the ones we use to prepare for our driving test. Therefore, it's not a waste of time to look around and find out what the market offers as far as these types of books and then purchase the one you like best.

These exams are often made by the panel of judges only a few minutes before the test begins. This is to keep the questions on the test from seeping out and falling into the lap of a candidate before the test, as well as to avoid favoritism or special favors among friends or neighbors, etc., who could give away the questions if they had been prepared beforehand.

This tidbit of information is more important than it seems. I explain it in further detail in the section on "Using Your Intuition to Answer on Competitive Exams."

B) THE SCANTRON OR COMPUTERIZED type. With these tests, you are given a form to fill out. Using a pencil, you have to mark the correct answer by filling in a space between brackets. These are the most common, in general, on competitive exams prepared by national organizations and also those in which there are a large number of candidates, because these types of exams are easier to correct, because they are done by computer.

Given the massive number of candidates who take these exams, they are usually prepared ahead of time, and therefore you can generally find more "malicious" questions on them, as well as more people with "connections."

We should know what kind of multiple choice test we are going to be faced with. Does anyone think that they are the same? Well, they aren't at all. There are certain subtle differences between them (although few), which we will look at ahead.

Using Your Intuition to Answer on Competitive Exams

A) If the exam is of the **mark-the-correct-answer-with-a-circle** type (format type A), we should expect each option to come up approximately the same number of times in the end.

For example:
- 20 answered with option a.
- 18 answered with option b.
- 21 answered with option c.

Keep in mind that these exams are often prepared *under certain time restraints*. If the exam begins late due to the fact that the jury is still creating it in the last moment, this will be more than enough to prove what I was saying before about these time factors and about how each option (a, b, c, etc.) will come up the same number of times in the final recount.

Remember how we said that if someone writes the letters a, b, and c quickly and without thinking, for example, one below the other, and then adds up each letter, almost always, the number of times that each of the letters come up as the answer is uncannily similar.

The speed at which these exams are often made reinforces this theory.

B) If the exams are **computerized** and the probability is mathematically favorable, we should risk it just the same. You have to keep in mind everything we said about the options appearing the same number of times, although this may not work as well because, in general, these exams are made well in advance and, in principle, we are more likely to come across the "maliciousness" that we had referred to before.

Nevertheless, I remind you that statistically, we will always be playing it safe with our answers, thanks to the use of our formula, which means that we have nothing to fear.

Plus, who hasn't heard of champion's luck? Isn't it a fact that you are going to be studying from now on like authentic champions? You will be champions!

CHAPTER 6

USEFUL ADVICE

It is much better to study **a little bit every day**, or almost every day (even if you only review or work on your weak points), than to cram from time to time.

It is a good idea to **rest for five to 10 minutes** every 30 or 40 minutes when studying, and 10–15 minutes every hour. This gives the subconscious time to assimilate and organize the information. Plus, it will be easier to be motivated and concentrate knowing that, every half hour or so, we can take a relaxing break. We can use these breaks to have a cup of coffee, a soda, or a snack, take a walk, or simply relax. However, it is not a bad idea to change rooms or atmospheres and forget completely about the work. No mental reviews, even if you feel you should. It is better to hold off and create a sort of "addiction."

The room we study in should be **well-lit**. Watch out for reflections caused by the light on books or papers you are using, because they can quickly tire our vision and thus lessen our concentration. Sunlight is always preferred.

We have to study with **our back to the sunlight**, which by the way is the best light of all, so that it shines on our work. Electric light is best from the ceiling; this way it covers everything and is dispersed more uniformly. It is not advisable to use a flex lamp because it produces more fatigue on our eyes, given its so-called brightness-loss gradient. For example, if we have one on our left, we receive much more light in our left eye and that pupil will be more dilated. On the other hand, the right eye receives much less light. This imbalance produces premature fatigue and could provoke headaches.

We should study **in a comfortable position**. Normally it is preferable to sit rather than to lie down, in order not to tire our neck muscles, arms, etc. Being too comfortable could also provoke sleepiness or asthenia. We will all discover the best position to study in. Also, we should make sure that our clothes are comfortable and proper for studying.

Try to study, as much as possible, in a **quiet room**, free from noise and interruptions.

Avoid **distractions** (radio, television, etc.). It is completely untrue that we study better this way. Studying is like watching a film at the cinema: We won't understand the film as well as we should if, for example, while we are watching, we plug some headphones in our ears and listen to some music.

When outside forces create **unfavorable study conditions** for us, it is better to review or take a walk and leave it for a better moment. However, be careful! Let's not fool ourselves into not working and turn this into a common excuse.

Before beginning our study session, it is a good idea to **have all your material at hand**: summaries, mind maps, pens, markers, blank paper, etc.

It is not a good rule of thumb to memorize **after a main, heavy meal**; it is better to rest at this time, or at most, review.

On the contrary, the best time to memorize is **after getting up and having a light breakfast**. Also at mid-afternoon, if we are awake. It is preferable to review at night; although, as we will see further on, any moment in the day is good for reviewing.

This means, for example, that it would be a shame to review in the morning, given that it would be a **waste of mental energy**, unless everything is already memorized or we don't have the material to be memorized in that moment.

When preparing competitive exams with a series of theoretical tests, and only if we have enough time beforehand, **we should start by studying the topics that will be on the final tests,** because the final selection of those who have passed will come from here. Remember that the psychological factor on these final tests is most important here, and as we advance through the exam. Our nerves can play the worst tricks on many aspiring test-takers at this time. Therefore, the more prepared we are, the better.

Thanks to this tactic, the topics we have memorized and learned for the first tests on the exam will be fresher in our minds, because we have studied them last. On the other hand, between each test on the total exam, we will have a few fantastic days to thoroughly review the topics on the theoretical exams we have left and that we will know so well!

Academies and schools? Due to the time lost in commutes, talking about football or other things during class, and going at a slower rate in general (in most of them), I **only advise this to those candidates who really need it.**

Except for a few quality schools that do indeed exist, it is always preferable to study independently and ask a private teacher or specialist about any doubts or questions we may have.

The Morning of the Exam

The best is to begin your day with an **energetic breakfast**. I also advise this to those who never usually eat breakfast. This is the best because we have a long day of intense mental activity ahead of us.

You have to leave enough time to arrive at the examination site without being in a rush. If we are strapped for time we will be provoking an unnecessary state of nervousness.

Statistics show that students, above all those taking competitive exams, get into more traffic accidents on test days. Therefore, **we must go to the exam early and without haste**.

Sometimes it is necessary (or at least advisable) to go a few days ahead of time, and know exactly where the exam will take place (when dealing with a competitive exam or the like). You should do this not only to find the building, but also the exact location of the rooms where your test will be held.

Large institutions can be tricky for students, who can get confused or even lost trying to find their room. This could result in arriving late to the exam (some can't find the room at all) and, furthermore, getting more nervous than necessary.

It is also a good idea to know how we will get to the test location. Are we going to walk? By car? How is the parking around there? How long will it take to arrive? These questions, for candidates who take their exam very seriously, cannot go unanswered.

If you were to **get in an accident**, you must contact the examiners as soon as possible and explain what has happened (logically, if the circumstances allow and nothing serious has happened to you).

The later we show up at the center where the test takes place (or took place), we should bring some type of written justification: from a doctor or police officer, or some other way that certifies that we have been in an accident.

If the accident were more serious and we can't go to the exam, someone should go in our place, with proof of our admission to the hospital, clinic, or wherever we are being treated.

Make every effort to be alone, **in peace and tranquility**, a few minutes before the exam. This is a time when we are apt to see many nervous people, impetuously reviewing their material, and where we will, of course, see other candidates laughing or joking around. The best is, without a doubt, to avoid all of them.

Finally the time will come when **the doors open** and the room where the exams are taken is open, giving way for the students to enter.

Once again, you have to try to control yourself and enter the room with optimism, without any sort of psychological pressure, ready and willing to take the exam and enjoy it. Don't finish it before it even starts. After all, we are the greatest specialists in the world, aren't we?

If we can **choose where to sit**, the best choice is in the middle of the room (from front to back) and against the wall opposite the windows. This is normally not possible to choose, either because the places are already established ahead of time or because we have come in the room too late (or too early) and they assign us a seat.

Pay close attention:

Near the windows, we can be bothered by noises outside, the sun and changes in temperature, which usually happens on a cloudy day when the sun goes in and out of the clouds.

In the back of the room we can be bothered by proctors that come in and out, if the door is located there, plus the air currents and noise from the hall.

In the front of the room, we will see that the proctors who are watching us are noisier than we expected and can sometimes even talk to each other in the room.

The place where I advised you to sit before, the temperature and light that we receive tend to be more stable. The sun won't bother us and the noises are farther away, even those from other students, who we will hear breathing nervously, dragging their feet, coughing, etc.

If we are sitting against a wall we will have less people around us, and therefore less noise.

Notice the layout and evaluation of the different seats in the following diagram:

Window	Aisle	Teacher
Sun and noises		**Worst places**
		Bad places
		Mediocre places
		Good places
		The best place
	Entrance	

If we end up obliged to sit **next to the window** (something that is possible due to the aforementioned causes) and the sun bothers us, no student should be afraid to close the window, and lower the blinds or close the curtains as needed.

If this is not possible, because there are no curtains, for example, it is best to kindly and politely ask the proctor for permission to change seats.

Remember that they won't get offended by this, and it is most probable that they are even happy to help you.

Next to the windows we will always be exposed to **more noise** from outside, due to construction, traffic, people walking by, etc.

Under these circumstances or the like, again, ask the proctor for permission to change seats. If we do this politely, it is not likely that they will say no, because it is something quite natural to ask.

CHAPTER 7

MEMORY AND OUR HEALTH

General Advice

- A balanced diet, without overdoing or lacking in anything, will help us with any activity we carry out in life, physically and mentally. Therefore, studying and memorizing are no exception.
- When we sit down to study, we should neither eat too much, nor eat heavy foods or foods that are difficult to digest.
- Of course cigarettes, alcohol, and any other type of drug will always be detrimental to us.
- If we study in the afternoon, it is better to save room at lunch and *later snack on something that we like*. This clears our minds as we take a break.

- It is not a good idea to memorize after a main meal; it is better to rest or, at most, review.

What Vitamins and Minerals Do Our Brains Need Most?

As for minerals, mainly **phosphorus** and **magnesium**, and as for vitamins, **A** and **D**.

PHOSPHORUS is found in milk and milk products (*be careful with cheese*, as it can cause migraines in people who don't tolerate it), eggs, whole-grain cereals, nuts, chocolate, and legumes (chickpeas, peas, beans, lentils, and soy).

MAGNESIUM is found in unrefined sea salt, whole-grain cereals, nuts, chocolate, and legumes.

However, in order for the body to assimilate phosphorus, it needs *vitamin D*. This vitamin is found in cod liver oil, and we also produce enough in our skin when we get some sun.

VITAMIN A is found mainly in animal livers and, outside of meats, in carrots, parsley, and sweet potatoes.

As you can see, there is not much more to say about this. A Mediterranean diet, for example, is very complete and really gives you all the vitamins and minerals that you need.

CONSISTENT, MODERATE PHYSICAL ACTIVITY, is very desirable, because it clears and relaxes our minds. Doing exercise tones our bodies and improves our blood flow, which is also something to think about and appreciate.

Finally, I would like to stress the importance of getting enough rest and sleep. We should try not to get overtired. Besides not being as productive this way, we create bad vibes, which make our minds unwilling to do whatever activity we want to do.

CHAPTER 8

PSYCHOMETRICS

Psychometric tests are becoming more and more frequent on competitive exams. They also often appear as part of the interview process for certain job positions. Furthermore, they often provoke a feeling of terror in many people who have to take them. They get the feeling that the situation is out of their hands, and that they can't control it. Sometimes they don't even understand correctly or don't quite know what they are being asked to do on the test or how to answer them. In other words, they feel lost.

This is why I have decided to include these tests in this book: to introduce them to you and help you pull apart the "mystery" behind each one of them. As you will see next, these exercises are neither strange nor magical—rather, on the contrary, they are usually pleasant and fun to do.

You may already know them and may have done them on some occasion. Even so, I advise you to take a look at the upcoming pages, because you can always learn something new.

These exams or psychometric tests can be classified basically into two large groups:

The ones intended to **measure a person's intelligence**, or their intelligence quotient (IQ).

Personality tests, based on the search for a determined psychological profile or personality balance, which meets the certain requisites of a particular job position.

We are now going to start by looking at the first group. You will see that there are many practical examples and then some exercises that you will have to do on your own.

Intelligence Tests

These tests are made to evaluate the intelligence of the person who is taking them.

They use different scales to measure the intelligence quotient, the most famous of them being the "Cattell Scale." Other scales that are used include the Terman, the Stanford-Binet, and the Weschler.

In relation to the IQ of each person, we can establish the following classifications:

EXTREMELY LOW
0–24 POINTS. PROFOUND RETARDATION (AN ADULT AT A MENTAL AGE OF 2)

25–49 POINTS. SEVERE (MENTAL AGE OF 3–6).

50–69 POINTS. MODERATE (MENTAL AGE OF 7–10).

BORDERLINE
70–79 POINTS. THEY CANNOT STUDY AT AN AVERAGE LEVEL TAUGHT.

Low Average
80–89 POINTS. THEY CAN FOLLOW THE AVERAGE LEVEL, BUT WITH SOME DIFFICULTY.

Average
90–109 POINTS. 50% OF THE POPULATION.

High Average
110–119 POINTS. TYPICAL AT A UNIVERSITY LEVEL.

Superior
120–129 POINTS.

Very Superior
130–139 POINTS.

Near Genius
140–159 POINTS.

Genius
160+ POINTS.

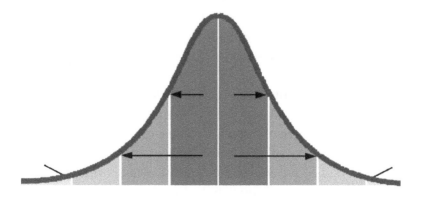

We cannot precisely measure quotients greater than 200 points, for lack thereof. They are only estimated.

The International Society, *Mensa*, only accepts "intelligent" members. There are more than 20,000 of them, and around one quarter of them have a score higher than 155 on the Cattell scale.

These IQ measurements are very important and considered in countries that know how to calculate them, like in the United States Highly gifted United States children often have important advantages for study, for example, being given scholarships or accepted into the best schools.

All of the systems created to measure intelligence have the same goal: to know a person's capacity to reason and find a logical sequence in a series of problems previously and precisely created for this purpose.

By taking a sample, using standardized tests with thousands of people, and keeping their ages, sex, level of studies, etc. in mind, they create tables or scales that are organized through careful mathematical calculations. Finally, they get a statistic that allows them to know if a person is more or less brilliant than the average.

For example, a person with 130 points is more brilliant than 90% of the population. If he or she had 148 points he or she would be more brilliant than 98% of the population. By the way, this percentage (98%) is what you need to get into *Mensa*.

The objective on these tests is to look for, by means of a series of calculated exercises, the end or the continuation of a logical sequence, which can be made up of numbers, geometric shapes or any other kind, etc. Once we find the rule behind the sequence, we can rationally jump from one figure to the next, all the way to the end.

The tests can also deal with sequences of numbers or letters, dominoes, "intrusive" vocabulary words, etc., although when vocabulary is in the mix, we cannot get a real IQ because luck can play a part in this and, in fact, often does.

The objective of these tests is to see if the person taking them has the minimum required intelligence.

The best secret I can tell my students is to be extraordinarily prepared, and have no weak points. That's why you have to know and practice everything that in some way could possibly be necessary in the future, even if it isn't now.

Let's look at some examples of the most common intelligence tests.

Numeric Sequences

These exercises consist of a series of numbers that are related to each other in such a way that, if we know what that relationship is—what rule takes them from one number to the next—we can continue the numeric sequence or chain indefinitely, adding as many numbers as we like.

Let's look at the most basic and simple example of this, seen in this sequence:

1, 2, 3, 4...

What number would come after 4?

First of all, you have to guess what rule this sequence follows. In the previous example, it couldn't be more simple. The rule is to add one each time, so the next number would be 5.

Likewise, if the chain were to count backward:

8, 7, 6, 5...

What number would come after 5?

The rule this sequence follows makes it so that the next number in the sequence is one less than the last—that is, they decrease by one each time—so the number we are looking for would be 4.

Numeric sequences, just like any other psychometric test, usually go in order of difficulty. So, if we get stuck, it would be best to forget about the more difficult exercises and go to another section on the test, to do the more simple ones in that section.

At the end, and only if we have time, we will go back to the more difficult problems the second time around.

Keep in mind that there is usually an abundance of time given to take these types of tests. Actually, there is more than enough time, so this doesn't really factor in the results.

In the following sequence:

4, 7, 10, 13...

What number would you write next?

We can see that the numbers increase by three each time, so, logically, the next number would be 16.

The next sequence is a bit more complex:

3, 4, 6, 9...

What number comes next?

It is not difficult to find the rule behind this sequence. We can see that the interval between each of the numbers in the sequence increases by one each time. So, if the difference between 6 and 9 is three, then the next one would have to have a difference of four, which would be 13.

In the next example:

4, 3, 7, 10, 17, 27...

What number would come next?

Notice how 7 is the sum of 3 + 4, or, the two numbers before it. Also, 17, for example, is the sum of the two numbers before it, 10 and 7. Therefore, if we keep following this rule, the next number would be the sum of 17 and 27, which is 44.

Look at the next example:

2, 6, 14, 30...

Which number comes next?

If we multiply a number by 2 and then we add 2, we get the next, so, the number we are looking for is 62 (30 × 2 + 2).

Let's continue with the last sequence:

3, 4, 8, 8, 23, 12, 68, 16...

What number would follow?

Now, this example is more complex and its difficulty lies in the fact that there are two different interleaved sequences in the same chain. Look at it like this:

3, 4, 8, 8, 23, 12, 68, 16...

The first sequence is made up of the underlined numbers. The rule that we have to follow to get the next number is multiply by 3 and subtract 1. So, we have: 3 x 3 = 9, and then, 9 – 1 = 8, the second number in this sequence, which is underlined. Then do the same with this one: 8 x 3 = 24 and 24 – 1 = 23. If we do the same with the last number in this part of the sequence, 68, we would get: 68 x 3 = 204 and 204 – 1 = 203, which is the number we are looking for.

The second sequence in the chain previous is an intrusive sequence, which is interweaved with the main sequence. Unless the exercises tells us otherwise, we should only give the next number in the chain, which would be 203, as we have seen before.

Nevertheless, and to finish this last example of numeric sequences, we can see that the second sequence is the result of adding four to each number, so the next number in this sequence would be 20 (16 + 4).

If the exercise had instructed us to give the next two results, they would be 203 and 20, in that order and the chain would then look like this:

3, 4, 8, 8, 23, 12, 68, 16, 203, 20...

And so on, to infinity. As you can see, they aren't difficult, and the trick is to guess the logic behind each sequence that makes the numbers appear successively. Finally, you have to be careful not to make a mistake when you calculate or carry out any other operation.

Dominoes

Of course you don't have to know the rules of this famous game in order to solve these problems. Just like we did on the numerical sequence problems, we should only reason out the rule or rules that make the logical sequence possible, and allow for the addition of more dominoes.

These tests are often used on some competitive exams, because they offer very reliable and objective results. That is why we are going to pay special attention to them in this section.

In the first place, it is fundamental to realize that each domino has seven different possible *faces*, which go from 0 (the blank one) to six. These possibilities are doubled because the possible results will appear twice:

- One above and one below, when the domino is in a vertical position, like the numerator and denominator of a fraction.
- From left to right, if the domino is horizontal.

Likewise, the two numbers on both parts of the domino can coincide, like, for example, 3/3, which can be considered *double*. If the domino is not double, then its numerator and denominator will not be the same, and it would then be physically different if we were to invert it.

Remember that in this last case we are talking about *different dominoes*, and it is necessary to know the correct order that its digits are in.

The dominoes can go in *increasing or decreasing* order, and it is of utmost importance to know that we can go beyond the number 6. From 6 we would then loop back to the blank one, or 0, and so on, forming *infinite circles*.

Look carefully at the following domino sequence. Pay attention to some of the characteristics that I described previously:

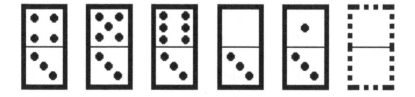

You have to find the domino that corresponds to the blank one shown on the right with dotted lines, which you should never confuse with the double blank piece.

In this first example, which by the way is very simple, we can see that all of the denominators are the same. So, logically, we must assume that there is another 3, as the final denominator, on the domino in question.

The numerator, however, increases by one as it goes. Notice how it forms the infinite circle we talked about, because when we get to the highest number possible on the domino, 6, the next number has to be 0, closing the circle. Then it goes to 1, and in this example, would continue on to 2, which is the numerator we are looking for. Therefore, the domino we are asked to give for this answer is 2/3.

Look at the second example:

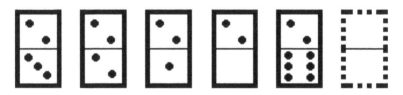

In this case, contrary to what happened in the first example, the numerator is always the same, 2, and will logically continue to be the same on the last domino in the sequence, the one we have to figure out, marked by the dotted line.

The denominator decreases by one each time, getting to the 0 or blank domino, and as you can guess from the previous example, it can continue descending. Remember that we said that the dominoes form infinite closed circles. In this case, a new circle would start with the number 6, after having descended to 0. After six, would come 5 and, therefore, the domino we are asked to guess would be 2/5.

Here we go with the next example:

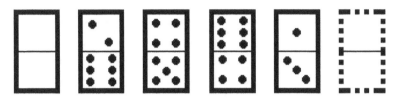

In this case we find ourselves with a numerator that increases by two each time. Once again (and as usual) when we get to 6, the highest number we can represent on a domino, we have to keep increasing, logically by 2 more (to 0 and then 1), and then again, which would make 3 our final numerator.

In the denominator we see a simple descending sequence that decreases by one each time, which should end with the number 2. So, our final answer would be domino 3/2.

Once again, in the next example (similar to the last one), the numerator increases by one each time. Therefore, the answer should be 0 for the numerator. Meanwhile, the denominator decreases by two each, and therefore would also end in 0. In conclusion, the domino that we are looking for would be the double blank domino, or, 0/0.

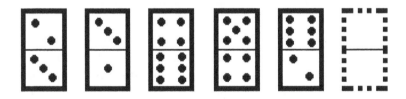

Let's look at this new and different example:

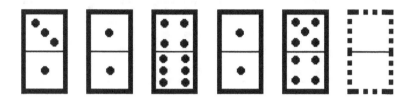

In this case we can see that there is an intrusive domino, the 1/1, which appears interleaved in the series and would thus be the answer they are asking us for.

The other alternate dominoes make up a sequences whose numerator increases by one and denominator decreases by two, forming a future 6/2 in this case. However, I do remind you that they don't ask us for this figure, so we don't have to write it down. At any rate, it is good to know.

Let's look at another example:

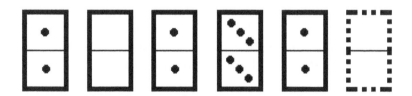

Don't let yourself get confused by so many doubles.

Here we have another case of an intrusive domino, once again, 1/1. On the other hand, we see a different sequence of dominoes, alternating with the 1/1 dominoes. This one is really the result of adding three to both the numerator and the denominator, which would mean that the next domino in the series, and our final answer, would be 6/6.

Here's a new example:

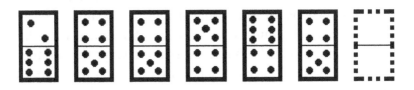

We see here another case of intrusion, which is produced by the existence of two different alternating sequences. In the first place we can see an increase by two in the numerators of the first, third, fifth, and logically the seventh dominoes, the seventh being the answer we are looking for. On the other hand, the denominators of these dominoes decrease by one each time: 6, 5, 4... and we can assume that the answer would have a denominator of 3. The answer will finally be 1/3.

Domino 4/5 makes an alternating sequence with the one above (which gave us the answer). Watch how it is transformed into its opposite, 5/4, and then back again to 4/5, back and forth, successively.

Next we will look at a similar example:

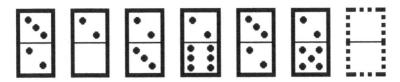

In this case, the even dominoes are not one intrusive one; rather, they make up a sequence. The odd dominoes (the first, third, etc.) is domino 3/2, inverted successively, alternating with the dominoes that make up the second sequence. The last domino, and the answer, is 2/3.

It is good to always make an effort to understand the second sequence when you are practicing, even though they don't ask us for it, because it is good training. We can see the second sequence here is 2/0, 2/6, 2/5. It isn't difficult to guess that the numerators are always the number 2 and the denominators descend by one each time. So, in this sequence, the next domino would read 2/4.

Let's continue on with another example. Spend a few seconds trying to get the results yourself. If you want, you can jot it down right in the book, on the empty domino:

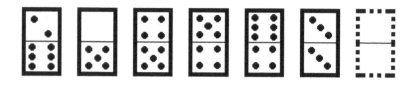

Notice how, again, there are two different sequences. On one hand we have dominoes 1, 3, and 5, plus the answer, the outlined blank domino in the seventh place. Here, the numerators go up by twos and the denominators, however, go down by one each time, giving us 1/3 as the answer.

The alternate sequence is made up of the dominoes in the even places. The rule here is that the numerators decrease by two each and the denominators by one, which would mean that the next domino in this sequence, *the domino they don't ask us for,* would be 1/2.

Study the next example and write down the answer:

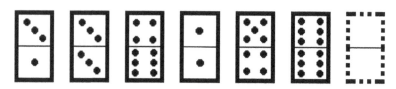

In the odd sequence, made up of the dominoes in the first, third, and fifth places, and the blank one corresponding to the answer (or, the seventh domino), we can see how the numerator increases by one each time and the denominator decreases by two, which would make the last domino, and the answer, 6/2.

The sequence made up of the dominoes in the even places has all double dominoes whose only digit decreases by two each time. Therefore, the next one in this sequence would be 4/4.

It's easy, isn't it?

Solve this new example:

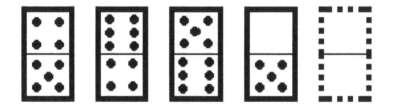

The first thing that should grab our attention is that there aren't as many dominoes in this one.

When there are only a few, you should suspect that there is only one sequence.

Did you come up with the answer yet?

Okay, here's the solution. Notice how the numerator on each domino is the denominator on the next, and the denominator plus one corresponds to the numerator of the next domino. Therefore, the answer we are looking for is 6/0.

That was easy, right? It is a question of practice and also using a bit of imagination to solve these problems. However, these sequences can get terribly complicated.

My goal here is not to show you every possible case, for that would be impossible. I only want to familiarize you with them and with the most common sequences.

Solve the following example:

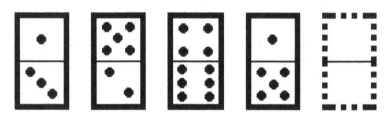

This one is similar to the one we have just seen. This time, if we add 1 to the numerators, we get the denominator of the next domino. If we add 2 to the denominators, we get the numerator of the next domino. Logically, the answer is 0/2.

A new example:

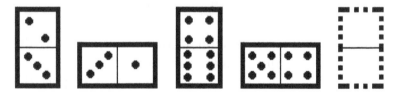

Don't let the horizontal dominoes scare you. The vertical ones are read from top to bottom, and the horizontal ones, from left to right. If they were too complicated for you, you could always mentally lift them back up, to the right, clockwise. On the horizontal dominoes, the numerator corresponds to the number on the left and the denominator, the one on the right. The numerators increase by one each time and the denominators decrease by two on each, so the answer we are looking for is 6/2.

Here's another example:

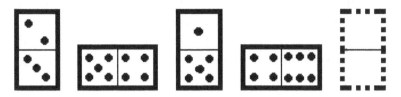

In this case you can see how the numerators increase by three, and the denominators increase by one. The answer is not too hard to find. It is 0/0.

The dominos can also appear on exams in pairs:

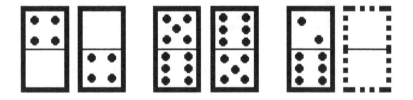

In this example we have three pairs and a logical rule that helps us move from the first domino of each pair to the second. I have made the first one simple:

The dominoes are "crisscrossed." That is to say, the numerator of the first one is the denominator of the second, and the denominator of the first is the numerator of the second. Therefore, the answer is 6/2.

Notice how the rule that allows us to go from one domino to the next is the same for all three pairs.

Let's see what happens now:

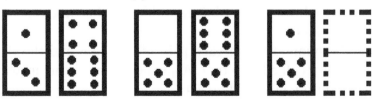

Once again this is about finding the relationship between the two dominoes in each pair, which will be the same and invariable for each pair in the set.

If we subtract 2 from the first numerator, we get the second denominator. If we add 1 to the first denominator, we get the second numerator.

Therefore the answer is 6/6.

Look carefully at this next example:

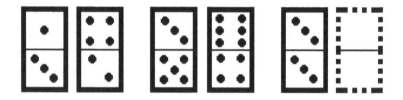

We can see that these dominoes are paired up in a way that the second numerator is equal to the first numerator plus 3. If we subtract 1 from the first denominator, we get the second. So, the result would be 6/2.

Go over this next example, which will be a bit more complicated to solve:

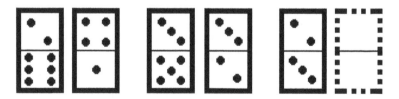

The solution was a bit more hidden, but not too difficult to find.

The numerators in each pair add up to 6 and the denominators all add up to 7. Applying this rule, the answer in the third pair would be 4/4.

The problems where the dominoes appear in groups of three can be a bit more tricky.

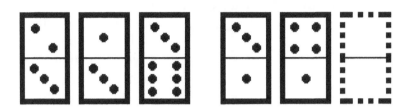

In this case the solution is much simpler than what it may seem. Can you do it?

All you have to do is add the first two dominoes in the trio (the numerator plus the numerator and the denominator plus the denominator) to get the third number respectively. The resulting answer would be 0/2.

Notice how in the second pair, the sum of the two numerators equals seven, thereby amounting to more than 6. Don't forget that we have to loop back to the 0.

Here's a similar example:

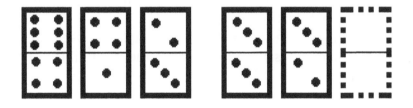

All we have to do is simply subtract (just like we added in the example before this) to get an answer of 0/1.

Problems like the following can seem more complicated at first sight:

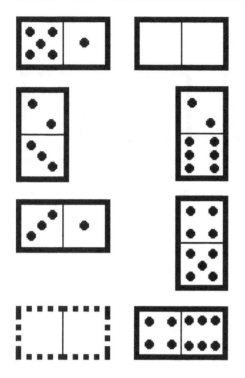

This is a spiral that starts with domino 3/1, which as you can see, is horizontal.

It might be easier if you imagine that each domino is a car traveling in the direction of the last domino, the answer. Each "car" (like all cars) has a front end, which in the first case would be a 3, and a trunk, or back end, which would be 1. The front ends of the cars decrease by 1 each time and the trunks, or back ends increase by 2. Therefore, the final car—excuse me—the final *domino* would be 3/1.

Let's go finally to the last example on page 189, which is like a mosaic and seems like the most difficult of them all.

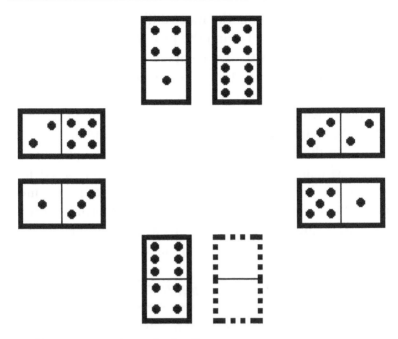

Can you see the solution?

The four horizontal dominoes (the ones lying down) are like a mirror image of each other. Notice how the two exterior numbers, the 1 and the 2, are in the same position on each side. However, the inside digits, the 5 and the 3, have been inverted.

Now you just have to apply the same rules to the four vertical dominoes. So, in order to find the missing domino, you have to keep the exterior digits the same, in this case, the 4 and the 5, and then proceed to invert the interior ones.

The result should be 1/5.

Once we have done the most difficult part, which is to find the rule or logic behind the problem in question, then all we have to do is try not to make a careless mistake on the easy part, which is doing the calculations.

We could also get confused and change the order of the digits without realizing it, thereby inverting the result of the final domino, which would logically end up in error.

In the exercise section you will find a few more of these, with an answer key, so that you can keep practicing.

Finally, let's continue with the last type of psychometric test exercise in this next section. These problems tend to scare some people at first, given the way they are designed. These are known as diagrams.

Diagrammatic Tests

First of all, it is important not to let yourself get intimidated by this name (or by any other, for that matter), because we have to have some name for these inoffensive types of exercises.

You are going to see a series of squares. We have to figure out the logic behind them. With these, we will conclude this section—however, not without reminding you first that you will find more psychometric exercises at the end of this chapter, so that you can practice solving them and enjoy yourself for a while.

Which one of the diagrams that follow (A, B, C, or D) corresponds to the blank one, in the dotted lines on the top row?

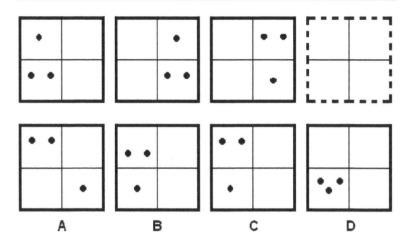

Have you guessed it yet?

The answer is C. Look at the evolution of the one black dot, which moves around the square clockwise, and the two dots do the same, counterclockwise.

Be sure you don't get confused with B. It presents the same distribution as C, but the two dots appear at the bottom of the square, not at the top, where they should be.

Let's look at another example. Take a few moments to try to guess the solution on your own.

If you want, you can try to predict it. Try drawing it in the book without looking at the four possible options.

If you have trouble, look at the options. The correct answer is among them; select the one you think is correct.

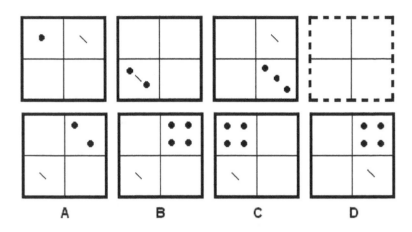

We can see that a new dot appears each time, as they change from box to box counterclockwise.

The dash jumps back and forth diagonally between the same two boxes, which are the ones that make up the right diagonal.

The only diagram that obeys this logic is B.

Solve the following example:

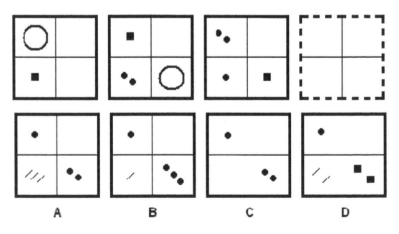

First look at the circle, which goes down diagonally to the right and then disappears. The rest of the shapes appear in the lower left box, go up to the upper left box, and then go down diagonally like the circle did, and finally disappear.

The only diagram that follows this pattern is A. C could never be it because no new shape appears in the bottom left box.

Here's the next example:

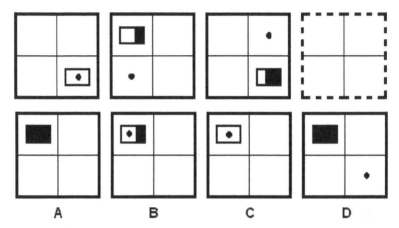

In this case we have a rectangle that alternates diagonally between the same two boxes, upper left and bottom right, and at the same time is gradually being filled in. Also, there is a dot traveling, apparently arbitrarily, around all four boxes.

The correct answer is A, where the two figures coincide in the same box. The rectangle is filled in completely and covers the dot.

Once you have finished these examples you can go on to solve the problems you find on the next pages. Then, check your answers in the answer key. Have fun!

Exercises

Numeric Sequences

Complete the sequences logically. Write the answers in this book to make it more comfortable for yourself:

5, 8, 12, 17...?
3, 2, 4, 4, 5, 8, 6, 16, 7...?
4, 2, 6, 8, 14, 22...?
3, 5, 9, 17...?
1, 3, 11, 123...?
25, 21, 16, 10...?
8, 12, 16, 24, 32, 48...?
3, 9, 7, 4, 8, 9, 5, 7, 11, 6, 6, 13, 7...?
1, 2, 5, 14...?
46, 24, 43, 42, 37, 24, 28, 42...?

Dominoes

Find the domino that completes the sequence, just like we did in the examples before:

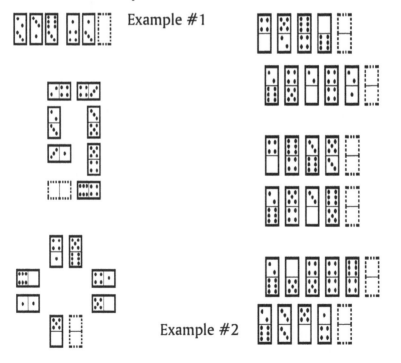

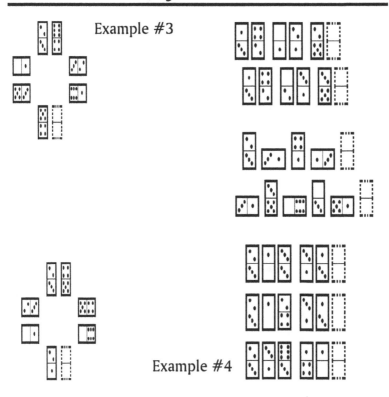

Example #3

Example #4

Diagrammatic Tests

Choose one of the four choices given below, A, B, C, or D, that completes the sequence in the problem above it:

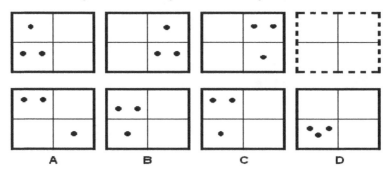

A   B   C   D

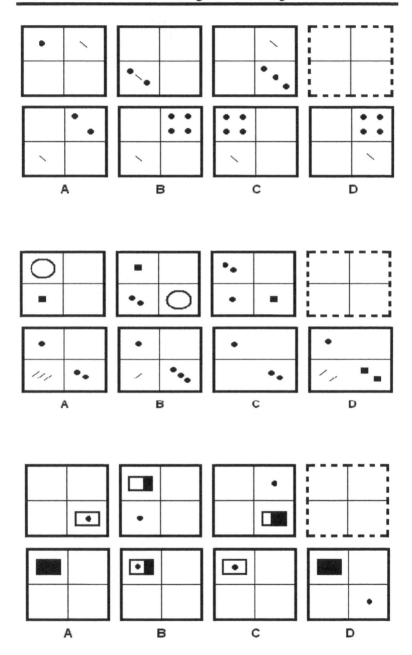

Answer Key

Numeric Sequences

1) 23   6) 3

2) 32   7) 64

3) 36   8) 5

4) 33   9) 41

5) 15131   10) 16

Dominoes

1) 1/1   7) 6/3   13) 1/0

2) 4/3   8) 6/4   14) 5/4

3) 2/5   9) 6/3   15) 5/6

4) 4/1   10) 5/5   16) 4/1

5) 1/3   11) 4/4   17) 0/2

6) 5/1   12) 6/2   18) 0/6

Diagrammatic Tests

D
A
C
C

Psychometric Personality Tests

These are made up of a series of quite unreliable questions designed to know the **psychological profile** of the person taking the test.

In principle, and as a general rule, you should answer all of the questions, but sometimes it is unadvisable to do so because it could lead to an error or incongruity.

For example, if they ask you "Do you like to ride horses?"

If you have never ridden one before, you shouldn't answer. We shouldn't confuse what we like with what we think we might like if we tried it.

Maybe then we see another question like this: "Have you ever ridden a horse?" If the answer is no here, you could be contradicting yourself if you answered yes to the first question, referring to whether or not you like riding horses.

There is a logical reason for this, and that is, if you have never ridden a horse, how do know if you like it or not?

People who answer that they like something that they have never tried before may seem foolish to the examiner (or to the psychologist who evaluates the test), don't you think?

These tests are filled with questions whose sole purpose is to find **contradictions in the personalities** of the test-takers. They may be like the question above or a question asking the same thing in a different way or repeatedly. These questions are often camouflaged among other trivial questions that are personal and transparent, like questions about tastes, for example. Evidently, no one can get a negative score on these tests, but be consistent with your responses. Don't say something different each time you are asked the same question.

Sometimes it may be necessary to "lie" a little in order to give off the impression or image they are looking for. For example:

- Those aspiring to be police officers should never say that they could lose their patience at work on certain occasions, even if it is sometimes true. Let's remember that they do carry a weapon, among other things.

- If the question is whether or not you would keep a wallet that you found on the street, supposing you did not know who it belonged to, the logical answer is, yes. What other valid option would you have? A negative answer here could indicate a childish personality.

- If we were going for a position in a nursery, to give one last example, and we had to pass this type of test we should say that we have plenty of patience and that we love children, even though we might be exaggerating a bit.

In general, this is also what we have to do in job interviews.

If you have any doubts, you should give the answer that you would like to hear if you were the one correcting the test, except with the aforementioned questions about personal tastes, whose only objective is to "fluff up" the test and gain the trust of the person taking it.

By the way, nobody should feel bothered by these recommendations or guilty for following them, especially on competitive exams, because all is fair in love and exams. The official organizations and their delegates are the first ones to "pull strings" for their friends and family when they can, so it's hard enough to get in as it is. So, unfortunately for some, and fortunately for others, competitive exams turn into a type of war, in which anything goes!

CHAPTER 9

PSYCHOLOGICAL PREPARATION

This section is not only dedicated to those taking tests, but to everyone, because life is one continuous exam. We are always fighting against something, looking for new objectives.

Let's take this exciting subject on as one of the most essential parts of this book. All the studying in the world or having the best memory would mean nothing if, at exam time, our performance was "ruined" by those darn uncontrollable nerves.

There's no doubt in my mind that, in order to be a champion memorizing, a champion studying any material or a brilliant test-taker, you also need a bombproof psychology, a psychology of champions—a high, rather, very high—self-esteem. There is nothing wrong with this; on the contrary, I am going to earnestly try to make all of my readers out there discover the secrets to making their fantasies become reality. I especially dedicate this section to those who need it most psychologically, and to whom I hope to infect with my enthusiasm, which is nothing more than the result of applying the following simple guidelines in my life.

Read this section carefully and reflect on its content. Then try to perform a self-criticism; that is, compare this information to your personality and the way you are, like this:

- What similarities and differences do you find between yourself and the different personality characteristics you have discovered?
- What are you like, and what would you like to be like?
- Are you able to feel enough affection toward yourself?

When you finish reading this section, come back here and answer these questions.

Exams

For the majority of students, exams provoke fear, if not panic. This real perception of fear is based on one supposed myth: **Failing is bad.**

Well yes, this affirmation is a mistake. Remember that we are talking about academic exams, not competitive exams. Failing is not bad, and it shouldn't even make us worry (in the strictest sense of the word). What would be bad, or at least cause for worry, would be not to study or to study poorly.

Nor can we really be 100% sure that it is always bad to fail a competitive exam. Normally, if we're talking about percentages, it would clearly be better to pass. However, how many people have ended up finding a better job, making their way down a new path, because they had initially failed that exam? The original mentality of these people: that seeing the word "fail" on their test results was something bad or the worst thing that could ever happen to them, suddenly turns into satisfaction. They realize that the worst thing would have been to pass and accept the job they were competing for in the first place. They discover, in hindsight, how great it is not to have passed. But, be careful! This happy ending, which in time has shown to be the most satisfactory, only comes to those who, due to their tenacity, didn't get discouraged back when they were faced with this apparent failure. Instead, with their hopes up high, they kept looking for new paths to take. I am not at all talking about those who, as they read this, find some pretext or excuse to voluntarily fail. Surprisingly enough, there are people who do this. Those who share in this mentality have neither tenacity nor self-esteem, and they are doomed to the most spectacular failure as long as they keep thinking and acting this way.

I don't want my words to be misinterpreted. Of course the main objective of all students, especially those taking competitive exams, should be to pass the exam—and the higher the score, the better. This is precisely why I have included this section on psychology in this book.

When students are taking exams, the last thing that they should be worrying about is the final result (in other words, if they are going to pass or fail the exam). A good example of this would be a person driving a car, worrying about if they are going to get to their destination alive and without having had an accident, rather than just relaxing and enjoying the ride.

When you take an exam, you have to let yourself get carried away with your hopes and enthusiasm (why not?) and enjoy it, just like you would with anything else that you get thrilled about. It's the best thing you can do. It's better for us to do this because, when faced with any amount of tension, our subconscious, using its defense mechanisms, tends to want to block out the information we have memorized, and that we now want to remember and bring into our conscious mind in order to be able to answer the questions on the exam. Even if our memory didn't get completely blocked, it could suffer some restrictions, depending on the actual state of nervousness we are in before the exam. Who doesn't know someone whose nerves caused them to suffer a mental block and blank out on an exam or the like, in which something important was at stake?

Even students who have studied the most or who have their material most solidly ingrained in their memories can blank out. These students have a burden of responsibility on their shoulders, and they feel they are under pressure to pass. This incredible responsibility they carry can become overwhelming. The main reason our subconscious can make our minds go blank is fear of failure.

When you are taking an exam, the die has been cast. At the exam, in that precise moment, we are no longer responsible for anything. We were responsible when we were preparing or not preparing for the exam, but at the moment of truth we shouldn't reproach ourselves for anything. We should relax, enjoy the exam, and let our knowledge flow naturally.

Fear of failure during an exam comes from the thought that failing is bad. Nevertheless, keep in mind that there is no such thing as failure for those who have fought with all their might. If we can avoid overrating exams and we stop associating them with success and failure, they will automatically stop making us afraid, which, in turn, means better results for us. I can assure you of this.

Needless to say, students who fail any type of exam and suffer from this will probably awaken fear in their subconscious. They are afraid, once again, of going through the same situation that caused this suffering. Notice how what I am now saying is that the suffering is not caused by the exam itself, but rather our personal opinion and evaluation of the results obtained after taking the exam. I am sure that this evaluation is nothing like the personal evaluations that other people have.

In short: There tends to be a state of alert, or even phobia, in the minds of the students who have chosen to excessively evaluate the possible results on an exam, even if they are waiting for the results of an exam that they have already taken (sometimes long before). This way, when they go to take the next exam, they will experience a fear that manifests itself as an infinite number of unpleasant physical sensations that are very difficult to control.

This fear is a direct result of their attitude. It is like a reaction to certain subconscious defense mechanisms. Your subconscious does not understand why you are there, suffering, and it wants to avoid this situation, or anything like it, in the future. Therefore, if you remember that you have an important exam tomorrow (or next week), you will immediately feel your mind disapprove of this in the form of uncontrollable nerves, anxiety, rapid heart rate, insomnia or any other unpleasant symptom. This is all for your well being, so that you don't go back to take another exam and to avoid repeating that ever-so-terrible experience.

Your subconscious really only wants to protect you (all phobias are defense mechanisms and ways of protecting ourselves that come from this "strange" subconscious mind of ours). It cannot understand how, just by answering a few questions (this is all an exam really is; the rest is just what everybody makes it into), you would put your health, self-esteem, and personal opinion of yourself in such danger.

Likewise, and with the exception of competitive exam candidates, when we are studying it would be wrong to think: Passing is good.

Passing or failing an exam is neither good nor bad. Maybe having to face a failure at some time in our lives helps us learn more for the long-term or near future. Maybe it helps us motivate ourselves more.

In the short-term it may seem good to pass exams at any price, even if we don't deserve it. But doesn't it seem more sensible to study with a good technique when we are students, master the preparation and memorization of the topics, and lose our fear of test-taking once and for all?

This would give us some fantastic years of practice, knowledge acquisition, and complete training that would undoubtedly open the doors to our future from one day to the next. This could happen by taking a competitive exam or by getting easy access to a job that directly reflects what we have studied, because we have become authentic experts.

In any case, thanks to our putting this into practice, we will become used to having a higher and better production level, and will have whatever it takes to get into the competitive labor market in our society or to simply continue studying.

Often students who just want to pass end up over-confident and too relaxed. They become mediocre and don't even come close to performing up to their maximum potential. Later on, they get poor results on competitive exams, even though they have academically been a "good student."

Be careful! I'm not saying that it is good to fail once in a while. Rather, the good or the bad lies in our technical and psychological preparation before an exam.

The act of taking an exam only means reaping what you sow, and, therefore, you shouldn't be looking for anything else at that time, and much less, miracles.

It has been proven that when responsible people fail an exam once, they look and find the causes of this "failure," learn from it, and strengthen their weak points. In the long run they obtain a much higher performance level than the conformist student who just passes without trying.

On the other hand, you have to keep in mind that there are other factors that influence the final results of an exam that don't depend directly on the student. Therefore, students can pass these exams in many different ways, which won't really benefit them at all in the future:

- Luck. Those who only study a topic or two, and luckily get asked about them on the exam.
- Copying. Sometimes the circumstances make it just too easy to do so. Who wouldn't?
- Lottery. Although if the students don't know at least a little bit about the exam, it would be really difficult for them to pass like this on a multiple choice test—more difficult than perfectly guessing or predicting every outcome in a football pool, blindfolded.

- Connections. This is definitely the exception that proves the rule. So many exams have been passed by "pulling strings," and so many will be in the future! If you have this possibility on an exam, don't doubt taking it; you'd be ignorant not to. I'm sure that other candidates would be glad to do it for you if you don't want to. Not to mention the times that you have lost opportunities on other exams you have taken because of someone else who had the connections, as well as the times this will happen to you in the future. And, on competitive exams, everything goes.

It is also possible to fail for reasons beyond our control. However, the chance that all of the necessary factors combine together, at the same time, to inflict such bad luck on us could only happen once in a lifetime, like winning some money in the lottery. Twice would really be impossible, unless we misuse our creative power to do so.

So, let's remember that the secret does not lie in passing or failing an exam, but in knowing how to prepare ourselves in order to face the whole process from the moment we start preparing the exam beforehand to the moment we finish the exam. It is also fundamental to know that we should treat ourselves with understanding and care after getting the results, especially if they are negative. This way we will bring out the best in ourselves for the future, and keep our dear subconscious from delighting us with one of its defense mechanisms: giving us a hand... right to the jugular!

The results will always come on their own, for sure, so don't worry about them. Simply face what comes, for better or for worse, and *we should then react and treat ourselves just like we would if this had happened to the person who we love most in the world.*

According to the aforementioned and to give an example: What should we do, or what should our reaction be, if we fail an exam?

We should react by feeling relaxed, loving ourselves, being our best friend in that moment, and treating ourselves as such. Talk to yourself and advise yourself with love! Have you ever tried it in front of a mirror? Well, I recommend it. Do it! When you walk away from the mirror you will see that something inside of you has changed for the better. You will feel relieved and liberated. Repeat it as often as you need to, until all the love and caring you get makes you become "an indispensable person in your own life."

Also, you should of course study and analyze all of the factors that have influenced this apparent "failure." Finding the cause of this will certainly help us know ourselves better and know how to prepare ourselves better for the exams that we have to take in the future. Working this way, you ensure that your failure will be converted into future successes.

Of course we are not talking about "students" who fail over and over again because they don't study or because they do not want to prepare for exams. The ones who only and exclusively think about having a good time and couldn't care less about anything else. These people need to grow up more and bravely assume the task of studying, as well as learn how to study.

By the way, who said that studying and taking tests aren't fun? Those who don't think so, especially about taking tests, think that you are risking too much when you take an exam, don't they? So then, what about dangerous sports? There are a lot of these, and the majority of people who do them are not professionals. They do them purely for fun. They are also risking a lot, aren't they? Nothing less than their own lives. They risk much more than someone who is taking an exam and only has a pen and an inoffensive piece of paper in front of them.

There's really no need to go to such lengths with such obvious examples, but aren't you really taking a test every day, from the moment you wake up? Do you not risk something every time you walk out your door, get in a car, walk across the street, or walk in front of a building? Am I wrong?

If you do things right and with love, everything can become quite fun. Plus it will give us some extra time to have a good time and enjoy ourselves in another way. You will learn to use every minute of your time living better and more joyfully, discovering wonderful feelings that will come to you without fail, from time to time, as a result of a job well done.

Students who know how to enjoy their work completely are not afraid of the final result. If we do not fear this final result, we will all bring out the best in ourselves and bring out our best abilities, which will make us enjoy ourselves even more. We get caught in a vicious, vertiginous circle of constant improvement and progress.

I think this is something worth trying.

Exams Are Necessary

If this weren't the case, how many of us would study? Let's be honest.

Without exams, many people would not even know how to read or write correctly, much less know any topic in depth.

All students must understand and accept that all types of exams are necessary. If we can understand this, we will learn to love them and see them as something good that forms part of our society, even though sometimes they are not done fairly.

Exams are necessary because they obligate us to study and learn, to be more competitive, and to be more prepared in the future. They separate or select those who make an effort from those who don't, the most responsible from the least responsible. It wouldn't be fair to measure everyone with the same yardstick, and out of false "solidarity," to allow everyone to pass, everyone to have a diploma, certification, or undeserved job position, regardless of the quantity and quality of the knowledge or aptitudes they have demonstrated.

What type of society would we be creating in that case?

Well, I'll tell you; a lazy society, without preparation, without any standards, and without any specialized professionals. Why bother if we all get the same in the end?

I'm not even going to go into the global results and consequences on our society (which already doesn't work too well) that would come over us, like rain from the sky, on every level (economic, political, etc), because that would be getting off track completely.

So, let's welcome academic and competitive exams as important and necessary, without misperceptions and without only looking at their most negative side, which sometimes does show. Let's enjoy them! But be careful! We also have to prepare for them!

Influence of the Psychological Factor

The psychological factor can normally influence our performance on an exam, making it vary between 60 and 90% of our maximum possible performance level, not counting basic information that we all have ingrained in our heads like, for example, writing our first and last name.

It is also not out of the ordinary to find much lower percentages in performance, which can even go as low as a mere "0"%. This would be the case of students who, due to the extreme nervous tension or extreme psychological pressure they put on themselves, end up with vomiting, diarrhea, dizziness, anguish, abnormally rapid heartbeat, chest or stomach pain, and many other symptoms. Some even get to the extreme of having to walk out on the exam or not even showing up to take it.

A certain percentage of these people can "get in over their heads" and may develop phobias from having so much fear. They may need specialized help overcoming these problems. In my case, more and more people come to my personal consultancy complaining about these problems, presenting one or many of the possible symptoms, devoid of hope, unable to concentrate, and with no self-esteem. In these cases, proper treatment is necessary before they crumble and completely fall to pieces.

When faced with an important competitive or academic exam (the psychological factor does not have as much influence on less important exams), we can basically find three personality types, regarding the degree of subject matter preparation and their performance:

A) THE SUPERPREPARED. These students represent about 2%, and the psychological factor (p.f.) can reduce their maximum theoretical performance to 80 or 90% of their total performance.

They usually have enough confidence in what they know, and some even have a lot of confidence in themselves. As a general rule they are "on top" in competitive exam tests as the partial results are posted. A high percentage of them will come first on the list and get the first jobs.

B) The Slightly Prepared. and especially those who go to an exam relying on luck. I'm referring to the ones who really have this intention, not the ones who prepare as well as they can and then say that they are going to "see what happens" in order to justify themselves to everyone else in case they fail. This is only a means of hiding all of their fears.

This group represents around 20% of all of the candidates, and their p.f. can reduce their theoretical performance also to 80 or 90%, because they don't have so much at stake and they know it.

C) The Average Prepared. Without a doubt, this represents the majority of aspiring candidates, in which the aforementioned p.f. reduces their performance, on average, to 60 or 80%, because they know that they are on the border between being chosen or not. They therefore place a lot of responsibility on themselves and are really the ones who suffer most. In fact, almost all of them usually have a bad time or really bad time, even if they get good partial results. Because the exam continues and they see a small ray of hope from their partial results, they feel even more responsible, and with that comes more psychological pressure.

Also in this group are the candidates who have absolutely no performance, due to the causes I mentioned before that are related to the excess psychological pressure and responsibility that they place on themselves.

NOTE: I OFTEN USE THE TERM "COMPETITIVE EXAM" OR I MAKE REF-ERENCE TO THE CANDIDATES. THE REST OF THE ACADEMIC STUDENTS, OR THOSE WHO AREN'T TAKING COMPETITIVE EXAMS, SHOULD NOT FEEL LEFT OUT HERE, BECAUSE THIS ALSO APPLIES TO THEM. COMPETITIVE EXAM CAN-DIDATES ALSO TAKE OTHER EXAMS, WHEREAS ACADEMIC STUDENTS DON'T NECESSARILY HAVE TO TAKE COMPETITIVE EXAMS. WHAT THE TWO DO HAVE IN COMMON IS THAT THEY BOTH TAKE EXAMS, FROM THE MOST IMPORTANT AND MOST SIGNIFICANT (COMPETITIVE EXAMS) TO SMALLER COMPREHENSION CHECKS OR QUIZZES TAKEN THROUGHOUT THE SCHOOL YEAR.

THEREFORE, BY REFERRING TO THE COMPETITIVE EXAM CANDIDATE I CAN INCLUDE ALL STUDENTS WHO HAVE TO PREPARE FOR ANY TYPE OF EXAM. IN THIS CASE IN PARTICULAR, THE DIFFERENCE LIES IN THAT, FOR THE STUDENTS WHO AREN'T TAKING COMPETITIVE EXAMS, THE PSYCHOLOGICAL FACTOR WILL BE LESS IMPORTANT. HOWEVER, FOR MANY, FACING ANY EXAM CONTINUES TO BE A TERRIBLE EXPERIENCE.

Psychological Preparation Phases

Psychological preparation must go through three phases:

1. PREPARING THE SUBJECT MATTER, memorizing it, and re-viewing it. This is the longest phase and is where the p.f. has the least influence. Furthermore, it can even have a positive influence. This happens when candidates motivate themselves by dreaming about passing, and creating their own hopes and dreams. They say things like, "Look how well I'm doing!" or "If I pass it would be fantastic because...!" and other similar expressions. This, by the way, is really good to do. In this phase students unconsciously consid-er that the "danger" of facing the exam is still far away, and therefore, there is enough time to react and become well prepared.

2. As the date is approaching. In this case, the p.f. already has a negative influence. It seems that we start to lack time and that what we know dances around in our heads from time to time. The information we have memorized doesn't seem to be engrained enough. This will indeed be true if there is already an excess of emotional tension.

3. The moment of the exam and the hours before. Sometimes even days before. It is the be all and end all. Real or even imaginary illnesses can appear. Suffering caused by excessive psychological pressure can become extreme.

This psychological pressure is normally at its maximum a few minutes or seconds before the test itself starts, and with this, our qualities diminish.

Nevertheless, what is interesting is how, a few minutes after starting the exam, if we have stoically survived the emotional pressure, our nerves calm down quickly and considerably. We often end up reproaching ourselves (at the end of the test) for having been so distraught at the beginning, and saying something like this: "I can't believe I suffered so much, and for what? The exam was a breeze!"

If that weren't enough, we usually still worry after the exam. In this case, we check and see that our friend's answers coincide with ours, and if they don't, we might think that we are the ones with the wrong answers. Now we have another reason to suffer.

This situation can get worse if we lose confidence in ourselves and there are more exams to come, as is often the case in competitive exams.

In our case, the first key to good psychological preparation is to **prepare for the exam conscientiously**, as much as humanly possible, because sometimes we don't have time or the means to prepare well enough. In this case, we shouldn't go to the exam suffering or anguished either. Nothing more than that.

Proper preparation implies doing this with time—not only because that way we have more time to study, but also because we will be more relaxed throughout the study process, which will allow us time to carry out other recreational or leisure activities.

In the case of competitive exams, it is better to study the subject matter and prepare for the exam even before the exam is announced. We can do this with subjects and topics from past exams, and we can work with the material that we know will be on the exam. Think about how, thanks to doing this, we are sure to pick up further knowledge that will be a great complement to the subject matter of the exam we will be taking.

This way, when the exam we are interested in is announced publicly and officially, we will already have acquired enough knowledge to move quickly and confidently through the final subject matter without getting stopped up.

We will have saved a lot of time without even realizing it, which will help us be relaxed right from day one.

Our subject matter preparation should be complete and perfect long before we get to the second phase, as the exam date approaches.

Some Psychological Advice

Giving ourselves time to prepare will keep us from feeling overwhelmed and help us "enjoy" ourselves more, even in the moments right before the exam. If we work consistently and do a little bit every day, we will prepare our exam almost without even realizing it, casually and with pleasure (we may even find it attractive), also enjoying other things in life, which will make us think that the life of a competitive exam candidate is not as hard as it seemed at first. This mindset will psychologically strengthen us even more.

On competitive exams we have to keep in mind that there will always be outside factors that we cannot control, which can influence our luck in the end. Therefore, *if we don't end up passing, the world will not come to an end*, and we have to try again. The statistics tell us that a considerable percentage of students who are very well prepared, and I mean *very well prepared*, pass their exam within the first five tries. That's not bad, and even more so if we consider that there is an average of 30 candidates per position offered, which means that on a competitive exam that is given every year, for example, we would need 30 tries to pass it if we have an average preparation. That's why achieving this in five tries is really good. But, how much have the poor fortunate ones studied and suffered for this? Nevertheless, my students often get it on the first try.

Remember that the best strategy for taking a competitive exam and guaranteeing your future is to *climb up the exam ladder*, if possible, beginning with the exams in which more positions are being offered. On these exams, the "string pulling" is less influential, as well as the overall preparation of the candidates, which is proportionately quite lower.

If, on the other hand, we were to try for a competitive exam in which there were only two or three positions offered, most likely (given my experience with many hundreds of students) the posts have already been filled. I particularly consider that a competitive exam is very attainable when there are at least five positions being offered.

Once we have our future guaranteed, we can calmly continue with our climb, taking exams for other positions that are better or more interesting to us. As a general rule it could be quite harmful to do this backward—meaning, starting with an exam in which only two or three positions are offered, as I said before, because they may already have been filled beforehand. Besides ending up disappointed, we could waste a whole year.

Keep in mind that the difficulty in getting a spot in a competitive exam lies in *the number of openings* and not in the number of candidates, because if there are a lot of openings to fill and we are well prepared, we will also find a high percentage of candidates who can't even spell their own name. (My apologies to those who don't know how to do this.)

Always remember that *consistency is the key to success*, and all of the effort we have made will always be worth it when we pass the exam and obtain our goal. That's why we have to be consistent and study every day, because it is much better to do it in shorter and more frequent sessions than in longer sessions without regular reoccurrence.

Don't skimp when you prepare for the exam. Strengthen your psychological preparation by thinking about what you will have achieved after you pass the exam, but do this with dignity, never putting pressure on yourself.

Bring *at least two pens* to the exam. The higher the quality, the better, because it would be quite bothersome if the pen doesn't write well or you have to furiously scribble on a piece of paper to get it to work before the exam. There is always someone with this problem on every exam, scribbling those invisible circles and finally asking anyone who will listen for a pen to borrow, because theirs doesn't work.

While we are on the subject, I remind you that it is best to use a blue pen, especially for essay exams, because the light frequency they reflect is relaxing (just like red produces excitement). This way, it is quite relaxing to see sheets of paper covered in blue writing.

You have to *understand the instructions correctly* and have absolutely no qualms about asking even the most simple question. Nobody will "remember your face" and then harm you. On the contrary, it is more likely that, if they favor anyone, they would favor the ones who ask questions politely and in a friendly way.

It is very important to realize that in order to achieve close to 100% of your maximum performance you have *to go to the exam as if it were nothing*—as if there were nothing at stake. We have to go as relaxed as possible, and with as much self-esteem and confidence as we can.

We should never feel or show any sense of embarrassment, mainly because this really doesn't exist. "Making a fool of ourselves" is a personal evaluation, not a universal opinion nor is it real. *We also should not be afraid* of any of the proctors or examiners. However, remember that they always like it when we treat them with the utmost respect and politeness.

While we study, and above all after making an intensive effort, *we have to know how to value ourselves personally and reward ourselves.* We also have to be patient with long, tiring activities or ones that don't give out very positive results, because a student's work, like any other activity, also has its difficulties.

Effective students require a *high dose of self-esteem* and self-confidence, as well as will and consistency. At the same time they have to do everything possible to get rid of their fears or complexes. I am sure that you are starting to figure out the best way to do so.

We should learn to *admit our mistakes, without any problem* and our errors, because we learn much more from them than it seems. Do not hesitate to start over again when you feel that it is necessary to do so.

When we are studying *we have to try to concentrate* on the topic at hand, whatever we are doing at the moment, and solve or set aside any problem, physical or mental, that could effect our performance. This is quite easy to do if we are using an effective study technique.

As we begin to study, and above all if our subject matter is long or complex, we should try to *charge up our patience and go step by step*, even though it may seem that we have a lot left to do or that we are hardly advancing. It is a thousand times more profitable to engrain everything well into our minds, going step by step as you have learned to do, than to go through the subject matter quickly, building castles in the sand (remember the story of the three little pigs).

We shouldn't put too much trust in all of our candidate colleagues—only in those who we are really sure of—because many of them can have a negative influence on us due to their lack of technical or emotional preparation.

Practice *sophrology techniques* to get over or improve any aspect of your personality whenever you need to.

Underneath it all, we should *long for the arrival of the exam date*. This is similar to what happens to race horses on the race track, when they are in their boxes, impatiently waiting for the race to start.

Avoid talking and making vain or inappropriate comments to other people—especially in the case of competitive exams, where we have nothing less than our future at stake.

It is especially wise to ignore those typical pains in the neck who don't stop telling us how they couldn't study nd how they are here just to give it a go, or those who tell us their whole life story (some even brag about having spent the night before out partying). They do this, the whole time laughing and making jokes, hoping that we go along with them and compliment them on their "great merit."

In short, we must feel *mental peace*. Push out any thought that does not provoke this and replace it with thoughts that do.

You have to go into the exam on *autopilot* without analyzing or thinking about what you are doing. It is another good way to control your nerves.

Finally, remember that, if we suffer too much from our nerves, *our subconscious will take defensive measures* to avoid our suffering. Why not? It will "help" us ever-so-kindly with a mental block or the like, so that we leave the exam because we are suffering, in order to stop feeling it. Isn't that just great?

Probably, our nerves will also want to be noticed physically, with a last attempt to "help" us. They delight in tormenting our stomach, our breathing, etc. Your subconscious will, in short, want to evaluate and protect you, depending on how far you have evolved lately in this aspect. It is its way of asking you: "Are you really comfortable where you are and with what you are doing?"

Feel happy, smile, and, using this feeling, say to your inner self: "Thanks, buddy, but today I feel safe and confident, and I don't need you to protect me from anything."

Control and Relaxation Techniques

People who know how to solve their problems are intelligent, don't you think? But, aren't the ones who know how to avoid problems even more intelligent?

According to what I have just said, the correct thing would be to learn self-control and relaxation techniques the day of the exams and the days prior, in order to solve any problems of nervous tension (if there were any). But really, when people suffer a nervous crisis, it is quite difficult to achieve an acceptable state of relaxation. For example:

If you are really worried because you are going to take the practical exam to get your driver's license and your instructor, who is sitting next to you, realizes this and says, "Relax," you would probably respond, "I would like nothing more than to relax!"

From this we can conclude that it is much more important to avoid getting nervous than to learn to control our nerves. This would be a more intelligent attitude and, if you do end up getting nervous, it would hopefully be to a lesser degree, so that we can control our nerves more easily.

Controlling our nerves will help us to not suffer as much (or at all), and help us not lose our sense of security and confidence in ourselves.

This way we will also avoid risking losing the information that we have memorized, which an excess of emotional tension could cause.

The famous saying "an ounce of prevention is worth a pound of cure" takes on great importance here. However:

When should we start to control our nerves?

For some, it will be enough to do this a few hours or minutes before the exam. Others will have to fight to not lose control a day before, and the rest will have to do this with even more time.

The important thing here is not to lose control in any moment before the exam. It is also quite true that if we feel nervous one or two days before the exam it will be pretty easy for us to control it. It is usually enough to focus our thoughts on something else.

The Nature of Our Nerves

Nervous tension appears when we feel **scared or frightened**. Nevertheless, we have already seen that we shouldn't fear exams. Rather, we should love them and accept them as something really necessary. If we are able to get rid of all of our fear and all of our worries, then we can't have any type of nervousness. It is a mathematical proof.

Underneath it all, as you know, our nerves are an instinct of self-defense. Our subconscious mind warns us that there is "danger" ahead, and so it places all types of impediments in our path so that we avoid this danger.

In any case, and until you graciously accept and find pleasure in exams and other embarrassing situations in life, which I recognize is difficult to do at first, it is a good idea to acquire some control and relaxation techniques as a means of extra help. You will soon learn these techniques in this book.

Even so, these control and relaxation techniques are like taking medicine to cope in a certain moment and under certain circumstances. If you need to take them it is because something is not right. The need to frequently do relaxation exercises is the same as depending on constantly taking medicine (this is just to give you an example).

Remember that an ounce of prevention is worth a pound of cure. Therefore, it is always better to look for and attack the causes that produce our discomfort or our illness. With nervous tension, we already know that these causes are: fear and worry.

So, let's attack at the base of the problem. We have to eliminate its causes for good, and then we won't have to ever take medicine again to control the symptoms we suffer from. That is, we will never need to use any relaxation techniques because we won't need to relax, because there will be no situation causing us to need it. We will always be calm and relaxed.

I must say to all of those who presume to know some good relaxation techniques and who use them every day, that I think that's great, but that something is going wrong, because they constantly need this "medication."

Even so, it is a good idea to save a "little pill" at the beginning, just in case, until everything is on track. Therefore, my advice is that you become quite familiar with the relaxation and control techniques that I am going to show you ahead.

The Fight Against Nervous Tension

The first thing that we have to do in our fight against our nerves is to gain *total control over our muscles*. In the very moment that we notice the symptoms that warn us that we are entering a situation of nervous tension:

- First, stop moving or making gestures, and let your body become completely limp and loose. Meanwhile, try to push out all of your thoughts and then, little by little, clear your mind, leaving it blank.
- Then, breathe two or three times, slowly and deeply, expelling all of the air that you have in your lungs. At the same time, you will start to feel your body get heavier.
- Notice how it is heavier and heavier with each breath and while you are pushing out all of the air.
- As you are breathing and your body gets looser and looser, you should then start feeling a pleasant feeling of well-being inside. Create it like this: "Nothing bothers you," "Nothing disappoints you," "You are starting to feel really good," "Better and better."

We have to mentally isolate ourselves from the outside world, feeling "better and better and better…" on the inside.

It is good to *practice* this technique a little so that we can do it naturally and not forced. If we are thinking about what we have to do to relax, WE WON'T BE ABLE TO leave our minds blank the way we should. Therefore, you should try to practice this every day, on any occasion, like any other exercise.

If your nerves show their ugly head during a **written exam**, it is best to:

1. Stop writing for a few seconds.
2. Do the aforementioned technique for about one minute.

If they appear in an **oral exam**:

- We should stop moving or gesticulating just the same.
- We should lower our voice and speak slower.
- We should discreetly get in a deep breath and relax our body as we let out all of the air.
- We should continue taking *slow, deep breaths*.
- We should think only and exclusively about the information we are discussing in that moment, *without any pressure*. Try to feel happiness inside. I guarantee that you will get surprising results.

In any case, we will be able to relax considerably in a matter of only a few seconds. In order to keep relaxed and gain confidence, we should continue with whatever we were doing, but only moving the muscles that are necessary to do so, without gesticulating or making any unnecessary movements.

We can also do quite a bit psychically. Don't torture yourself with negative thoughts or by thinking about things that have nothing to do with the test, like other people or about our responsibilities.

Fundamental

Never think, "I can't" or "This is getting out of hand." If you do, you will be lost.

We have to feel comfortable and remember that we are our own best friend. Really notice the company of your "best friend." If we are in such good company, then why worry?

CHAPTER 10

ALL ABOUT WORRY

Worry is the detonator of the worst problems in every society. Ninety-nine percent of the world's population lives in a continuous state of worry about something, and with the limits that this implies on the development of a good quality of life.

Normally, worry is closely related to the idea of "problems," and it surfaces when we over-evaluate the uncertain results of something that we are doing or are going to do in the future. We can also do this with someone other than ourselves, who we are interested in.

When I say "uncertain results" I am referring to the number of times the majority of people worry, for no particular reason, about things that haven't happened yet and are only castles in the sand. Who has never worried about something that they had to do in the near future, or about something that was going to happen to them, and when the time came, the things that worried them worked out just fine? So, our sufferer says something like, "Fortunately everything turned out much better than I had expected," or someone else comments, "See, you didn't have to worry so much."

This is because, underneath it all, worrying about something (furthermore when it hasn't happened yet) makes no sense at all and defies logic. Humans need to live in a world in which everything around them functions perfectly and is under their control. If this is not the case, worry pops up.

By no means am I saying that we should care less about everything—rather, just the opposite. This is precisely why we have to act at the right time, without worrying about the results, especially when they are so often uncertain. Quite frequently, the results do not coincide with what we were hoping for. They can even be the complete opposite of what we wanted. What then, when this happens? Nothing. Nothing happens, except for what we want to happen.

As always, we have to use our ability to choose. What do we choose to do, or who do we want to be when we are faced with the unexpected results that have disappointed us "a priori"? I say "a priori" because many times the saying "every cloud has a silver lining" soon becomes a reality. We discover that these "bad results" were the best thing that could have ever happened to us, or at least much better than what we had expected. Well, I was saying that, when faced with results that are contrary to our pretensions, results that evidently seem to go against our interests, we can always choose, even if it doesn't seem that way. We can choose the solution we feel is best for us, in every case. Sometimes it may seem that this isn't even a possibility and that there are no possible bad or really bad results, but rather, only one horrible one. Here, the best thing to do is apply the old proverb that says "If you can solve your problem, then why worry? If you cannot solve it, then why worry?" In these seemingly extreme cases we can always choose lifting our chins up or getting depressed, between handling it with dignity and class, or crumbling and despairing. Which of these do you choose?

When we are in a real serious bind, when we must never fail ourselves, when we need ourselves most. If something in our lives has gone "to pot" we have to know how to accept it with integrity, and dignity. The bad results have already happened, and all the suffering we do after that will only make the problem worse. If there is no solution, there is nothing more to do: either deal with it or rip it out by the root. However, and I insist, do it with class, dignity, and integrity, which all humans have, yet many do not know where to find.

Don't make yourself suffer any more, just as you wouldn't make your best friend suffer if he or she was the one with the problem. Give your intimate inner friend the best advice you can. Talk to him or her! Then pay attention to your own words and immediately put them into practice. There's no doubt that, if you always act like this, life will surprise you with compensations that are much greater than the damage you may have had to suffer in the short term. Above all, we are the creators of our own destiny, and our power to create circumstances goes well beyond what we can imagine.

One day a man came to my consultancy telling me he was really "burnt out" from work. He told me that everything there was bad because he had to get up very early and work many hours; he couldn't stand his boss; his colleagues, the work environment, etc.; and, to top it all off, he didn't earn much money.

"You are making this very easy for me," I said to him. "It is evident that the cause of your problem is work. Quit and don't go to work tomorrow. You will see how your problems disappear."

He replied, "What are you saying? I can't do that. I have a family and children, and they all depend on my salary."

I asked him if he loved his family, and he said he did immensely—that he loved them more than anything in the world.

So, because we did agree that, thanks to his job, he could keep everything that meant most to him in the world, his family, we came to the conclusion that his work had something good to it, even if it was only one thing. Therefore, I proposed to him that we draw a scale on a sheet of paper together.

On one side of the scale we put the negative aspects of his job, and on the other side, the positive. We then evaluated the results together—that is, which way the scale should tip; and the possibilities that my patient would then have.

On the negative side, we began to place his schedule, the hours he worked, and so on. He immediately started saying, "And this is bad, and that is bad too...," and we continued adding more and more weight: his boss, his colleagues, where he worked, his future possibilities, his motivation, salary, vacation time, days off, and so on.

It never ended. The tray on the negative side was completely filled with weights that represented the negative things. Then, with a mix between satisfaction and pride, he looked at me and said, "What? Isn't that enough? I have enough reasons to feel so bad, don't I?"

On the positive side of the scale, we put the weight corresponding to the financial independence that his work gave him: his salary, which provided for him and his family. Suddenly my patient added, "You can stop counting there."

I proposed that he evaluate the inclination of the scale, not by the number of weights on it, because it was clear that there were many more negative circumstances than positive ones by the actual weight of each of them. This, after all, was what really mattered and what would determine which way our scale would tip.

This man recognized again that he wanted to continue working, just as he had said at the beginning, because, although there was only one positive thing about his job—financial independence—this weighed more than all of the negative combined. This gave him the ability to have and maintain that which meant most to him and what he valued most: his family.

Finally, and in conclusion, I proposed that he do everything possible to change jobs—that he find something better. Nevertheless, in the meantime, while he *freely chose* to continue working at his present job, he should change his attitude toward it, for his own good and the good of his family. He should think about the scale and look at it as one unit, without distinguishing between the two trays.

"You have your problems," I told him. "But right now, what do you get out of carrying that burden with you every day by only considering the negative tray on the scale instead of looking at both sides at the same time? You are only looking at the tray that you yourself recognized as the one that weighs less. Concentrate for a few minutes only on the positive tray, for a change. Look at it! Think about what it says to you."

When he left, he made the proposition to try to change his attitude while he stayed in his present job. He would also take a close look at what the positive tray meant to him and start taking advantage of the time he has to spend with his family. Because he was going to continue working, he would make the best of it, because protesting and complaining wouldn't really help him change anything. Also, his suffering at work was the result of only looking at the negative tray on the scale—of a partial and unfair evaluation of reality and his ability to choose.

I did not prohibit him, at all, from looking at the negative tray again, when he wanted to, but I told him that, every time he did it, he should look at the scale as a whole that represents one indivisible and inseparable unit. I told him to remember which way his scale was tipping.

Wishing him a lot of luck I said goodbye, with hopes that he would soon find a better job.

Two months later this patient came back to my consultancy. Great satisfaction was written all over his face.

"Without a doubt you have found a better job," I said to him slyly.

"No, nothing of the sort," he answered. "I simply decided, in my greatest moment of despair, to change my attitude at work. In spite of still not accepting it, I looked at both trays on the scale, without breaking apart the indivisible unit, just like you told me to do."

He also commented that something like a small miracle had happened. Suddenly, as he changed his attitude and his state of mind, his colleagues' attitudes toward him had also changed. His boss valued him more and asked him where the other guy had gone (the one who never stopped complaining).

My dear patient realized the true power of words: They make us feel and create everything that we continuously express. We end up believing the things we say incessantly. He stopped talking negatively about his job and spoke more about the tray that weighed more. This new point of view, more fair and realistic, also improved his relationship with his family and circle of friends.

A few months later I ran into this man again, on the street. Without saying a word, he crossed the street and very decisively, almost bowling me over (he definitely was impulsive), gave me a huge hug. He insisted on treating me to a coffee. I remember quite well that I said to him, "Now I'm definitely sure you have finally found a fantastic new job."

"Nothing of the sort. My situation has improved greatly. My colleagues love me and I love them. My boss values me much more and now I have been compensated with a better schedule and more free time. I feel more important and furthermore, I am getting a raise. I even think—God! I would have never imagined—I think I even like what I do! And to think that this radical improvement in my work situation wasn't due to changing jobs; rather, it was due to my attitude toward it. By changing my attitude, everything has changed."

Notice what wise words came out of his mouth when he realized that he himself created his own reality.

Fortunately, this patient's (now a good friend of mine) attitude changed for the better. The creative power of our minds, our words, and our actions is enormous, but it is necessary to know that it does exist. Not knowing that we have it is bad enough, but using it in the wrong way is even worse.

Remember: Everything in our lives is limited to **what we choose to do or who we choose to be** when faced with any of the circumstances around us.

If our car gets a flat tire, we really have two options: Are we the driver who assumed this could happen one day, and therefore just grabs the jack, and maybe whistles a tune as we change the tire? Or are we the one who kicks the flat tire and punches the hood of the car and only to then shout, "Why do I have such bad luck?"

The problem was the same for both of these drivers: simply an unexpected flat tire. However, what defines each character and makes them different is really their attitude, and their ability to choose and think what they will do or say next.

The drivers who get mad will finally have to change the tire as well, anyway. It may take this type of person more time to do it, and given their attitude, it will probably be much more difficult for them. Maybe when they get back in the car, their foot hurts, or their hand or a finger maybe got pinched by some tool they were using or some part of the car while they were changing the tire. Maybe their foot hurts because they kicked the car to let off steam. Not to mention what a miserable time they will have had and the anger they must feel. Plus, there is the added risk that their anger may negatively effect their driving skills, perhaps placing them in an unsafe situation.

If we compare this type of person with the first type, the first type will have finished changing the tire well before the other, they will have done it safer and better, and they will simply continue on their way without any more setbacks. The whole thing will have been a small unforeseen occurrence that had been previously assumed as something that could happen. In short, this will end up being a completely irrelevant situation for them and they probably won't even tell anyone about it.

So, was the true problem for both characters the flat tire or their attitude toward it? Does getting a flat tire implicitly mean having a bad time?

Let's not forget that those who act out against themselves often do so in all types of situations. Due to this self-abuse that they constantly inflict on themselves, everything seems to go wrong for them, although it is also true that they will always get the results of what they create.

By the way, and talking about cars, allow me now to give you an example of how little use worry is to you. This is a case of premature worry.

Let's imagine a man, driving in his car on a 200 km (120 miles) trip between two cities called A and B. The driver should, if he uses his intelligence properly, try to enjoy the trip, stop if he is tired and take a walk, have a cup of coffee, or simply rest if he needs it, always feeling happy inside. He is, after all, the one who decided to take the trip. Furthermore, he is traveling with his best friend (he himself).

It makes no sense for our driver to set off on his journey worried about the final results of the trip. That is, he shouldn't be worried about getting into an accident or not, taking a curve wrong, not arriving to his destination alive, or crashing at some point on the trip. Don't you think?

Almost everyone travels by car frequently enough to see the logic in this, which in short, is that it is ridiculous to suffer thinking about the final result, and even more when the final result is uncertain. This means simply enjoying the trip and not worrying about the results, because they come on their own. Furthermore, many times the results don't depend on us and are beyond our control.

In the same way, it makes no sense for a student who is taking an exam to worry about the final results. This can be regarded as serious psychological self-abuse. Don't you agree?

What sense does it make for a student to be worried about passing or failing, instead of trying to enjoy the ride and have a good time answering the questions on an exam (just like playing a trivia game with friends). After all is said and done, answering questions is fun, especially when they deal with general knowledge. If this seems strange to you, think about how many game shows there are in which the contestants have to answer these types of questions. The audience also likes to participate by answering questions from home. What's so bad about doing it like this?

After reading this, many people could respond: "But when I am watching a TV game show or playing a trivia game with my friends there is nothing at stake. Nevertheless, on a competitive exam my whole future is at stake and depends on a few questions."

Well, it is precisely for that reason. What better reason to enjoy the ride? The facts and knowledge that we have to show on the exam are filed away or saved in our memory, in some corner of our subconscious. Yes, in the part of the brain that can sometimes play such nasty tricks on us if we don't understand how it works and if we don't treat ourselves with patience and understanding, and as if we were our own best friend!

Our subconscious does not understand why someone who is taking an exam (its "owner") has to suffer so much over it. It always wants to protect us. It's that simple. In order to carry out this mission, it has a number of defense mechanisms that can culminate into the appearance of what we call phobias, which I talk about later. Our subconscious won't doubt using these mechanisms if it means protecting us from a greater evil.

If we are too worried while we take our exam or do any other activity, our subconscious will do everything possible (which is always a lot) to keep us from doing whatever it is that is causing us to worry so much. It will communicate this to us by means of provoking different symptoms that are very unpleasant, and some quite hazardous to our health, as we have mentioned earlier in this book.

Our subconscious will even make our symptoms worse, to the point that we have to stop whatever it is we are doing as soon as possible. If need be, it won't hesitate to block access to our memory, for example, when we are taking a test when we have to speak in public. This way, it will once and for all stop the suffering and get its "owner" to go home immediately, to rest and recover.

Check it out! Underneath it all, our subconscious acts in response to a self-protection or defense mechanism, and to an order of priorities, in which the health of their "protected one" is most important (much more than answering some questions on an exam).

Our subconscious only understands feelings. It will ask you over and over how you feel about what you are doing. If you feel pleasure, good sensations; or good vibrations (as they say), your subconscious will want you to frequently repeat the actions that make you feel so well. If you have gone to the movies and you really enjoyed the experience, you will probably want to go again. The mere thought that you are going again today will make you feel good and will compensate for other bad moments you may have had throughout the day.

If you think about the last time you played a trivia or similar game with your friends, for example, you will notice how, when you were playing, you were living in the present and enjoying yourself answering some questions. As I said before, it can be quite fun. Nobody worries about winning or losing the game (except those who have some psychological problem). Much less would they worry a few days before playing the game, like they would in the case of an exam. Therefore, because the players feel comfortable and they only want to have fun and have a good time playing, their subconscious will do everything possible so as to keep them playing happily. Their subconscious will make it easy for them to achieve full access to their memories, to the point that if players are asked something that they don't know, their imagination will soar, and their memory, reflexes, and their whole mind will become as sharp as possible. Their subconscious will stimulate their faculties so much that oftentimes the players who don't know the answer to a question under normal circumstances, will guess the correct answer or at least come close. This is exactly the opposite of what happens when "the victim" of an exam transmits feelings of worry to their subconscious.

Also notice how these friends' memories aren't the only things that are heightened while they are playing the board game. Our subconscious can do even more to liven things up, so that they continue playing and having a good time. Perhaps it does this by taking away or at least alleviating a headache, or making them momentarily forget their problems, the bad day they were having, etc.

Here we can deduce that our subconscious not only is not bad, but its main task is to help us, even if this is hard for us to understand at times.

For our own good, we have this powerful tool to protect ourselves with. However, precisely because it is so powerful, we have to be more responsible when we use it, thus, never working against your subconscious, but rather, working with it, playing on the same team.

If we are suffering or having a bad time, it is because we have made an incorrect choice, one that hurts us. This is almost always motivated by having overrated certain things or matters to the degree that we become too worried about them.

This is why, if you want to get the most out of your mind before an exam, a job interview, or anything else in your life, you have all the more reason to enjoy the ride.

Feel good on the inside and enjoy what you are doing. Forget and stop worrying about the future and concentrate on having a good time doing whatever activity you are doing at the time. It is something that is really fun and worth your while. You won't regret it! Your subconscious will notice how comfortable you feel, and will do everything possible so that you keep feeling that way. It will sharpen your memory, your wit, and your mental faculties, so that you don't give up, and leave and so that you can continue taking those wonderful life exams, living out experiences that communicate enjoyable feelings to your mind. You will experience these feelings fully when you convert your subconscious into your best friend.

Once you and your subconscious are joined together this way, forever, nothing will be able to separate you, because no matter how "bad" things seem to be on any given occasion, your loyal friend will be there for you. Your inseparable subconscious will be there, ready and willing to help you, with all of its creative power.

It will always be ready for you, prepared to immediately and irremediably grant you with the fruits of your choice. I am also referring to the special circumstances that "miraculously" happen after the fact, which always work in our favor. They will end up making you think and feel that you are a lucky person. However, remember that, underneath it all and forever, you are the one who will choose, and everything will come to you as a result of the choice you make.

Phobias

It could be that, despite everything, our intrepid and inexperienced test-taker could fail the ever-so-important exam. What happens then? How should we react in this situation?

It is precisely when we apparently "fail" that we need ourselves most—when we have to be our own best friends most. What would happen if one of our friends failed the exam? What would we tell them? Isn't it true that we would say something like "Don't worry about it! You did the best you could" or "You'll get it next time" or something similar to make them feel better?

This is the right attitude to have with our friends. We put our arm around them, treat them to a cola, and give them some inspiring words.

If we are the ones who have failed (or something has turned out bad for us) we should work in the same way, making ourselves feel better, having a cold drink, and, why not, "celebrating" it (or perhaps you prefer the term "compensating") with a special meal we like. What is so bad about treating our friend to a nice dinner to compensate for the bad time we have gone through? I promise you that, after all of this, your problem will have become smaller and you will start to feel much better.

Keep in mind that, as I said before, our subconscious only understands feelings. However you feel about what you are doing, your subconscious will act accordingly in the future. If you turn a failure (or anything else in life) into a trauma and you suffer because of it, your subconscious will want to keep you from going through a similar situation and will undoubtedly take the necessary measures to do so. As your exam date approaches, for example, you will begin to feel bad. You will probably have digestive problems, sleeping disorders, or some other pathology. Your mind, being the unconditional friend that it is and will always be, won't want you to ever go through an experience like that again. You have created a phobia (or at least it has started). Like all phobias, this is based on fear, which, like all fears, begins with excessive worry, which, like all worries, originated from a bad choice or your overly negative evaluation of something.

If this is your case, you won't feel comfortable before an exam or before the situation that provoked this defensive reaction in your subconscious until your phobia disappears. However, it will only disappear when the causes that provoked them do and when you show your subconscious that there is no reason for it to protect you. You do this by changing your actions, your thoughts, and your words. In short, your new or changed feelings show it that it doesn't have to protect you, because now, your new choices do not generate any type of fear or worry.

This means that you should do everything within your power to pass, but at the same time, you shouldn't care about the results. When, and only when you truly feel this way, will your subconscious stop pressuring you and you will start to feel relieved. Your phobia will start to subside.

If, on the other hand you "stick to your guns" and allow each failure to affect you the same, the only thing you will assure yourself of, day after day, is to reinforce your phobia and make it stronger. Its symptoms will show up sooner, and more frequently and intensely. It will be more and more difficult to treat it because you will accumulate more and more unpleasant experiences. You may even get to the point of thinking that you are just like this, and that, unfortunately, there is no solution to your problem. Nevertheless, your opinion of yourself would be wrong because you weren't like that before. You were not born that way. You are simply what you have made yourself into—what you have decided to be.

That's probably not all there is to it. It also has a decisive effect on your self-esteem and the concept that you have of yourself. You may think that you aren't able to do this or that, and you will begin to develop frustrated feelings, which end up in an inferiority complex. If this complex becomes a reality, which usually happens quite quickly, you will find yourself caught up in a vicious circle which is hard to escape from. The more inferior you feel, the more inferior you will be in reality, and thus the worse you will feel as a result. This will go on and on until you truly break the cycle and radically change your attitude and your feelings about yourself.

Anyone who suffers from worry has their hands tied, and it quite often becomes something much worse: fear. People who live immersed in any type of fear lose their freedom. All arguments, conflicts, and wars have begun out of some type of fear. Fear pushes down our self-esteem, which is so important for a happy life. Among other things, fear lowers it and can even make it disappear.

If we have enough self-esteem, we will evidently support ourselves with love, under any of life's circumstances. It is ridiculous to love others, with whom we almost always have a provisional relationship, or who we see from time to time, and at the same time, "care less" about ourselves, even to the point of frequent psychological abuse.

People give advice to others. Everyone gives advice to everyone else, but, when the time comes to take action, when we need to act ourselves, we often forget the good advice we had so thoughtfully given to others. On the contrary, we often do the opposite of that advice. Where is our understanding now? What happened to the advice we gave to others, like "Relax, man!" or "Don't worry" or "You did the best you could" or "If you can't solve the problem, let it be; there's nothing you can do about it," and so many other similar phrases. These statements certainly carry with them the good intentions of lifting the spirits of the one we are trying to help, and we almost always achieve this. Therefore we can deduce that we are also capable of doing this with ourselves, because we have shown how we have the ability and the knowledge to do so with others. It should even be easier for us to help ourselves than to help others because we know ourselves so much better in every aspect.

In short, we all know what to do when faced with the problems we are dealt in life, or perhaps I should say when faced with the circumstances that we decide to label as problems to worry about. We know that the best way to behave is without worrying constantly. This is why everyone would like to live free from fears and worries.

I promise you that this can be done, and you know it. I am not telling you anything new; I am just reminding you; we all know it. So, we advise others to do it this way, to live without worrying about things, but if we are the ones faced with a problem, we make different choices and we let ourselves be led by rage, anger, or by any other similar feeling that can harm us. We let ourselves get carried away by our routines and customs because we are used to suffering, and it is the only thing we know. Although others should take things differently, we can't or we shouldn't, and we prefer to throw a tantrum and then let off steam.

Do you really think that our minds have such terrible limits?

Our minds only have the limits that we believe they have. In my consultancy, I often compare the power of the mind with the case where we are walking around with money in our pocket, without realizing it. Let me show you with an example.

Let's suppose that one hot summer day (like today, as I write this) you are walking down the street and you walk past an ice cream shop.

You get the sudden urge for an ice cream, but you think that you won't be able to buy one because you are sure that you have no money in your pocket. Let's imagine for a moment that you actually do have money in your pocket because two hours ago you ran into someone who owed you money and gave it back to you.

It all happened so fast. You were walking, the other person was in a hurry, and, on the fly, you stuck the bills into your pocket, but one that you don't usually use for carrying money. However, today was an exception and now you do have money in one of your pockets. In fact, who hasn't coincidentally found a bill in a pocket where they never expected to find anything, and therefore were given a nice surprise? Everyone has at some time found a lost bill in an unusual pocket, either because they changed it from their usual pocket that day, or perhaps because they were emptying out that pocket to find something that was deeper down in it, or for any other reason. Imagine, in this case, that you had your mobile phone in your good hand and you took the money that your friend gave you with the other hand and stuck it in a pocket that you don't normally use.

Let's carry on with our example.

Nevertheless, and despite having enough money on you, because you don't know that you have it (or don't remember)

you are convinced that you are walking around broke—
that is, with no money.

Therefore, even though you tend to walk a bit slower
as you pass by the ice cream shop and your mouth waters,
you don't stop. You regret "not having any money on you"
and you end up giving up, you keep walking, and you think
to yourself, "Maybe next time."

On the other side of the street, you have been spot-
ted by an onlooker. He saw how you slowed down as you
looked at the ice cream shop and how, at the same time,
you made the gesture of patting the pocket where you usually keep your change. By the way you were searching for
coins, the way you slowed down, the way you looked at
the ice cream shop, and from the look of disappointment
on your face, our onlooker guesses that you would have
liked to have bought yourself an ice cream, but you can't.
Our onlooker, who is sharper than a tack, keeps thinking
and finally comes to a double conclusion: "The person who
walked by the ice cream store wants to buy an ice cream,
but doesn't have any money; or, the person does have
money and doesn't know it. In either case, the person kept
walking."

So then, the way our onlooker correctly deduced and reasoned out the situation is the reality of our minds; it's our day-
to-day experience. There is no difference between a real no and
believing that the answer is no, even though in reality it is yes.

If we think that we are limited, we certainly will be.
Remember: If you think that you don't have any money,
you don't; there's no difference. If you think that it will be
hard to do something or you will suffer doing it, there's no
doubt that it will be more difficult to do or you will suffer
more than you should if you try to do it. The creative power of our minds is instantaneous here, and you will see its

immediate effects. If, on the other hand, you think that you can do something, every day—if you think so with courage, without obligation, without fear and constantly—it is impossible for you not to achieve whatever you desire. Where there's a will, there's a way. Consistency is the key to success. I'm sure you have heard expressions like these more than once. They are not only beautiful, but they are completely true.

History shows how many people have had an incredible drive and how, with that drive, they have obtained their goals, no matter what they set out to do, but they never lost hope and they never lost their motivation. On the contrary, they always believed in themselves, yet at the same time they didn't place unnecessary demands on themselves, even though they knew exactly what they wanted to achieve. They never worried about the final results, and they always treated themselves as if they were their own best friend.

On the other hand, other people push themselves to the limit in order to make everything in their lives work perfectly, so that they don't have to worry about anything. That's precisely what they do achieve: They live worrying about not having any worries. Even though this means great sacrifice for them, they try as hard as they can to be up to date on everything just to finish whatever they have started sooner or finish something that they have on their to-do list. They are really convinced that they will rest better when they have nothing left to do.

This is a possibility, but it is better to learn to enjoy our activities, the good ones and the bad ones, and it is good to remember that, if we choose to do them, it's because we believe that it is in our best interest to do so, even if we sometimes don't like it. Trying to make everything around us turn out perfectly is often such a big struggle and makes us suffer so much that, without a doubt, it is better to sometimes allow certain things not to turn out well. That way we can relax and eliminate some excess psychological pressure.

Of course, sometimes you have to be cold-blooded enough to allow, or even force, something to turn out "bad" in life, which can even bring some sort of reward with it. Even without the possibility of any reward, getting your accumulated worries off your chest can be reason enough to justify an apparent failure.

One time, a 15-year-old student came to see me with his parents. He had a problem at school, which is currently a very typical situation: He failed five subjects on his report card.

By the genuine look of panic in his eyes and from the results of the personal interview that we had, I came to the clear conclusion that this student made quite an effort to study and to pass, but he wasn't able to achieve it. Both of his parents agreed that he spent quite enough time with his books, although they didn't really know if he was concentrating while he was studying or if he was daydreaming.

During our session we came to the conclusion that this boy had one subject that stopped up everything else. He spent most of his time on this subject but never really ended up understanding it well. He spent so much time on this subject that he compromised the rest of his subjects. In fact, the ones he did pass, he did so by a hair. He seemed to be seriously psychologically affected by the relation between the time he spent studying and the results he obtained.

The best solution I could think of was that this student should stop spending so much time on the subject that was driving him crazy and worrying him so much, and then divide up the hours per week that he saved by doing so among the rest of his subjects. There was really very little to lose, because he was failing almost everything. By dedicating more time to the other subjects he could expect better results in all of them, not to mention the release of psychological pressure caused by the struggle with the subject he had difficulty with.

This seemed to us to be a very viable solution. I say "seemed to us" because when I proposed this to his parents, they approved immediately and were happy to see a possible solution. The student was most delighted when he realized that his only obligation to that subject was to not even look at it.

At the same time he and his parents could feel a bit guilty: Do you mean that we really aren't going to do anything at all in order to at least try to pass this darn subject? And herein lies the secret: not under the current circumstances.

We still had a loose string: What would the young student say to his teacher when he gets zero after zero in his subject, if confronted about the cause of this?

He should simply say that he is going through a bad time and, no matter how much effort he made, he didn't understand the subject correctly. He would say that he wasn't able to concentrate on it and that he felt that he was incapable of learning it. He would then add that he was suffering a type of mental block and therefore would ask the teacher to show him how to understand it well and how to study the subject properly.

No matter how the teacher reacts, the plan for the next grading period was already in place. The young student wouldn't spend a minute more—not even a second more—studying the subject that gave him so many headaches.

After some time, and once the next grading period was over, the young man and his parents came back to my consultancy, as we had planned.

By the look on his face, it wasn't difficult to see that something had changed radically. After looking at his grades, I saw, to my delight, that he only had one failure (nothing like the five that he had on his previous report card). We already expected that failure, didn't we? Of course we did, and logically it did not surprise us. How could it?

But the surprises kept coming. Without counting the failed subject, he had an average grade of B in the rest of the subjects, whereas before, he had only achieved a barely sufficient D in the subjects that he hadn't failed.

That wasn't all. His self-esteem had also increased considerably. Besides having an F on his report card, he was now a good student, as I see it, because in the rest of his subjects he had higher grades.

He told me that this was the first time he had enjoyed himself studying during the school year. He felt he had much more time, without the psychological pressure or an excessive feeling of responsibility, and that he was much more motivated to study. He even said that he liked it (sometimes), which was impossible and unthinkable three months prior.

He added that he especially enjoyed it when his teachers read his grade out in class, with a surprised look on their faces (just like his classmates), given such great improvement in such little time.

What was the secret after all? It's simple. He had to be cold-blooded enough to "eliminate" an important obstacle from his life that was holding him back continuously, harming him in his studies and in his personality development, and that had given him a false image of himself, making him feel inferior, even stupid or slow, and, of course, like a bad student.

With one failure he could pass the school year and not have to repeat it, which was his greatest fear. Finally he had to drag that subject along throughout the whole course and he decided only to make a small effort for a few days in the summer, studying and taking private classes in order to finally pass the make-up exams with flying colors.

He had managed to pull through the school year brilliantly. He now considered himself to be a good student, his complexes disappeared, and, better yet, he began the next school year willingly, with bravery and high hopes.

A radical change in his strategy was enough to quickly transform terrible results into brilliant ones. That same year this young man took one of my presential courses on study and memorization techniques, and is currently one of the most brilliant students I know. His majesty now "strolls" through every course he takes, year after year.

Sometimes the teacher is to blame for the student not understanding a subject correctly, although it is true that the majority of the time, the student is to blame. I am especially talking about subjects like math, which are not at all difficult to understand and therefore not difficult to pass, if they are explained properly. I am referring to teachers who right out fail almost everyone in the class, and I mean just about everyone. We often see a class of 30 or 40 students in which only three or four pass. Ironically, the majority of these students who get a private teacher later on, discover that Math is simple, and maybe even enjoyable to them, when before it seemed boring and detestable. When they really understand it, they say "That's it?" or "It's that simple?"

It is also true that the subjects they teach throughout the school year are too dense. It seems that our education system prefers to cram in too much of material, even though there is not enough time to cover it all as thoroughly as necessary, rather than consolidating the students' knowledge little by little. It is as if it weren't necessary to understand what they are trying to study.

Many teachers do not know what to do about this. They feel incapable of covering so much material in so little time. On the other hand, if they spend too much time on the student who understands the least about the content they are explaining, they will hold back the rest of the class and fall behind in the curriculum, only making matters worse. So, whose fault is it in the first place? Are both the teacher and the student victims?

I firmly believe that our education systems and government associations should legislate this. They are the ones that have the power to avoid these circumstances, which disappoint anyone who wants to study. These circumstances say so little for our national education systems, which is so easily demonstrated by the extremely high failure rates nowadays.

It would be much easier if students had much less material to cover in the same amount of time, and if they covered this material more slowly, and with more examples and more practical exercises.

In my opinion, the top priority is that the students learn something about what they are studying. On the contrary, what usually happens is that they get discouraged and scared by the number of books and amount of material that they have to study. In reality, the priority nowadays makes students fly through this extensive subject matter without understanding anything. It would be so simple to eliminate an infinity of useless information that they are obligated to study. Let the students be free to choose how they want to entertain themselves or waste their time later on, when the students are older and have finished their degrees.

A Personal Agenda

Personal agendas yes—the ones that have every hour on every page for planning out every day of the year—are simple instruments, that, without a doubt, are one of the most practical inventions for living in today's society. I would even say that they are "simply revolutionary." We are obligated today to plan numerous appointments and change those plans, over and over, so that we don't forget them. Remembering everything that we have to do, or better yet, the fear of forgetting this, is not at all good for us.

Having to remember numerous appointments, obligations, and an endless number of things to do becomes another worry in life: "Don't forget anything!"

There is nothing more worrisome than being worried about worrying about having to remember your worries! This is like the supreme worry. Our subconscious mind absolutely hates having to remember obligations, and also hates living in a state of constant worry over this.

Having an agenda means having only one thing to worry about: opening it every day, reading what is written in it, and acting accordingly. Once we close it we can disconnect without worrying. Every once in a while, our friend, the agenda, will remind us of all of the obligations that are imposed on us, even the ones that we have to start acting on, taking precautions, or just start preparing in general, as long as we have conveniently jotted them down.

An agenda is something like a guardian angel that comes to say, "Sleep tight. I'll take care of everything. Tomorrow I will be delighted to remind you of what you have to do. For now, disconnect and get some rest."

This powerful and, at the same time, very simple and economical tool is even advisable for those who have a relaxed life with no worries. The few worries they may have might be not forgetting to go to the hairdresser or wishing someone a happy birthday.

If you have never used one or it doesn't seem to be of much help to you, I suggest that you try using one for one or two months and then decide.

Write everything down in it. Get everything off your chest by telling your agenda in detail. Your friend, the agenda, has a lot to offer you and will never deceive you or leave you out in the cold (unless you lose it). Once you open it, you will easily remember what you have to do, which is simply everything you have chosen to jot down in it—just like that.

***

My dear friend, I hope that everything I have written here serves to help you in your life. I would love it if you used your mind, with all of its strength and splendor, for it is not in vain that it is our most powerful tool. Always feel good, want the best for yourself, pamper yourself, and treat yourself with kindness, consideration, and respect. Do not doubt that, this way, everything good will come to you. Furthermore, you will be able to help others easily, because you will give to them from what you have, and you will have so much to give.

This way you can't have any worries or any thoughts that effect you negatively, because when all is said and done, everything is based on our own choices. What I am saying to you is, choose! Always choose the supreme version of yourself. Choose what you would, for the person who you love most. If you discover that the choice you have made, or the thoughts you have had are not the best for you, change them enthusiastically for new ones, without any fear or hesitation.

Choose freely and without fear because your best friend, your mind, will always stand behind you and support you. Look at yourself in the mirror at home every day and talk to yourself for a few minutes. Tell yourself about what has happened with complete confidence. After all, you are telling this to the person who you love most and who also loves you most. Advise yourself then, and you will see that you are much wiser than you thought.

When you stop looking in the mirror and your best friend's reflection disappears, when you are no longer together and you go to your living room, you will see that something in you has changed. You will feel comforted and more free. You will have created this feeling for yourself. Your problems will have become lighter and easier to withstand. They may have even disappeared completely.

Do this wonderful exercise of meeting with yourself every day. Come back here and read these pages as many times as you need to, until you don't need to read them anymore, until this new experience that you have acquired transforms you into a genuine master of life. Do this until you turn into the master of your actions, your words, and your thoughts.

In order to do this, you have to unconditionally unite with yourself and throw yourself into the fantastic adventure of life, without fear and with high hopes. Remember: You choose.

CHAPTER 11

THE CREATIVE POWER
OF OUR MINDS

Who hasn't gotten a stomach ache (not to mention ulcers), diarrhea, a headache, anxiety, anguish, and so on, because of their uncontrollable nerves?

Each and every one of these physical sensations has been created by our restless and uncontrollable minds. These physical effects are completely real and are not in our imaginations, as many may think. The one who suffers the most and pays the consequences is our own body, at least at first.

What happens after we experience these bad physical feelings and discomfort?

When these feelings (or the experiences that provoke them) are repeated enough, they may even effect our deepest feelings.

And what can happen to us mentally?

Repeated feelings of nervousness or anguish can really limit us in our work, in our social relationships and, in general, in many daily situations. They can even give us complexes. Often these people can end up feeling inferior, thinking that they are useless for this or that and, finally, develop their own complexes.

Notice how, one "simple" mental act, in this case due to these uncontrollable nerves (or an erroneous interpretation of reality), can alone create real undesirable physical feelings and illnesses, like different aches and pains, ulcers, migraines, etc.

It is interesting to state how the creative power of our minds, is "better" at creating negative physical or psychic realities (mentioned before) than it is at creating positive realities. Why is this? Are we bad creators?

Evidently, we are not bad creators, and therefore we create at full force, although we mainly do this to create negative or harmful realities for ourselves.

Many people begin to psychically convince themselves that they have an illness that they really don't have. After some time, they have been able to make it a reality, and therefore experience it as such. Really, our minds have an incredible power of autosuggestion!

Okay, we are not terrible creators and we can even create physical realities only by thinking or imagining them. However, as it seems, if we only create negative things or harmful things for ourselves, then:

To what do we owe this apparent failure produced by our creations?

In the first place, we shouldn't call it failure, because we always create what we want to, even though it may take us time to get it. We also create what we fear or provoke, although we often do this unconsciously.

In second place, what happens is that we are not using our mental strength correctly. *Our mental strength* can seriously harm us, just like when we don't know our own physical strength, we cut our eye as we scratch it too hard. Our mind has so much strength, such creative power, so much energy, that it is better to make friends with it, friends with ourselves, 100%.

Some of us use this mental strength consciously, and many more of us use it unconsciously, not to mention those who don't use it at all, in principle, out of lack of values, criteria, or simply out of comfort. They simply let themselves get dragged along by popular conscience, by their ideas, opinions, and whims.

But, getting back to what we were saying, just like we can create negative physical and mental realities with our minds, we can also create positive ones. I would say that it is even easier; we have just become especially good at using our mental strength in the wrong way, and furthermore, we do this every day, which has consequently produced a real experience that works against us.

We are real experts at this. If we put the same energy into creating positive realities, don't doubt that we would achieve them just the same, or even sooner. Really, deep down we want more good things to happen to us than bad things. It's just that we often use our mental creative power in the opposite way.

The Keys to Our Mental Power

There are three of them, and they allow us to control our personality, our life, and even our destiny. These three personal modus operandi definitively make up our reality, and they are thought, word, and action.

Let's look at what happens. When someone *thinks* that they are unhealthy or ill (even if they really are at the time), they don't stop feeling sorry for themselves and they *tell* everyone how badly they feel, and socially, they also *act* accordingly. For example, they live their life apathetically, and they close themselves up in their homes, not wanting to go out, etc. The illness has been well-engrained into the mind (perhaps, and quite probably, it was also created unconsciously; there is a lot involved here). It is so fixed in their minds that if they continue to think and act this way, they will carry this burden throughout their whole lives, which, by the way, will probably be a life constantly lacking in the most important things, and full of suffering and self-torment. So, they continue this way until they firmly decide to change their mentality, the way they focus their life and, of course, act accordingly.

Some may be asking, "And if this person really is sick, due to outside causes?"

Let's put the cause of their illness aside for the moment. These people, and everyone else for that matter, should use their creative power in a positive way, for their own interests, and not use it against themselves, as they usually do.

Experts in Creating Negative Realities:

A) Constantly think that they are not well. They feel this way on a daily basis, and they look for indications and signs to show this is true. They are convinced that any change in their bodies or minds is for the worse.

You, on the other hand, must work to feel good every day and look for indications that you are well. Think that, day by day, you are improving your health, your work situation, your finances, the way you are, your social relationships, etc. No matter what you want to improve, you will end up making this real for yourself.

You should think and act this way all the time; don't think you are going overboard if you really have no doubts and are firmly set on adopting this mentality. Feel your inner confidence, as if an extremely positive energy were flowing out of you and is destined to achieve whatever you set out for. I'm sure that you can and will.

Don't give up. Don't change your mind. Keep your idea strong in your mind, every day, until your wish finally becomes a reality.

B) Tell everyone that they are not well. They don't stop saying this and therefore end up believing it more and more.

You, on the other hand, must tell the whole world how good you feel. Tell them that you feel better and more hopeful every day. You will end up creating and feeling this as your own precious reality.

C) Act apathetically, poorly, in a way that apparently confirms "how bad they feel," once again creating that feeling of illness in their minds, yet even stronger and more consistent.

You, on the other hand, act pleased and accordingly with what you want to be and create for yourself. You will end up becoming what you wish because you will have created this reality day by day, with each thought, each word, each gesture, and each act. All of this is created by you. You cannot ever think that you aren't what you set out to be, because you really will become it.

Negative people use their creative powers poorly or un-consciously, but they do it daily and consistently. This they do indeed do well.

You should do the same: Use them every day, continu-ously, but positively. Always look ahead because every day is a new world. Don't try to fix anything that you have and don't like, because that would mean looking into the past. Change it radically! Change your thoughts for new, better ones. Convert yourself into your best friend for real, every day, and help yourself and love yourself as you are. Create! This means looking ahead.

Move along the path of life, creating the best image of yourself—the supreme image of your persona. Do it con-sistently, with hope and with love.

Don't worry about results: **They will come** and will al-ways be favorable for you.

It can't be any other way.

INDEX

ABOUT THE AUTHOR

Professor Ramón Campayo is a professional hypno-therapist and one of the best mentalists in history. Mentalists are divided into three groups: memorization experts, arithmetic calculators (those who do adding, multiplying, roots, and other mathematical operations with an infinite amount of digits), and lastly magicians, who exclusively use magic tricks and their mental ability.

Ramón Campayo is the fastest memorizer of all time. On November 9, 2003, he shattered a total of 15 world records in speed memorization (three seconds) in Starnberg, a city in the southeast of Germany, near Munich. He beat every record possible (binary numbers, decimal numbers, etc.) in less than an hour! He has continued to defend his title as the fastest memorizer in the world since then. His most recent achievements include taking first place in the 2009 Open World Speed Memory Championships in Munich, Germany.

It is important to point out that serious memorization tests in international championships cannot contain text, due to the fact that it would have to be written in one language, thereby giving unfair advantage to natives of that language. However, by using numbers, each competitor is treated equally because these characters are the same for all of them.

Decimal numbers (that is to say, those between zero and nine) are the most difficult to memorize—more than binary numbers (used by computers and only consisting of zeros and ones). However, the latter requires greater precision of memory and more photographic acuteness. This is because, when the time comes to write the numbers down, after memorizing them, the competitor tends to confuse them. This can logically happen to anyone who tries to write long sequences of only zeros and ones.

Ramón has always enjoyed specializing in speed memory tests because he truly loves teaching others, not superficially, but rather by creating great champions. He has been sharing his study techniques for many years through his Website (*www.ramoncampayo.com*), and in the courses he gives all over the world and at his personal consultancy in Albacete, Spain.

So, what led Ramón Campayo to specialize in memorization speed? The simple reason is a logical one: Students are always working against the clock. It is good and necessary for them to learn to do things quickly. Obviously, this will allow students more free time to rest, have fun, or spend time doing other things. In other words, free time that will psychologically strengthen the student, proving that studying is not such a gruesome task (they really have a good time studying with the professor's methods) and that it only takes a bit of dedication.

But, in order to memorize quickly, in addition to technique, it is also important to read quickly. Ramón Campayo can memorize a **40-digit** binary number that appears suddenly on a computer screen, in only one second! A number like this:

01101001010110010110
01011010100101100011

One can suppose that, before memorizing this sort of number, he first needs time to read it. It is also not surprising that he holds world records in speed-reading, with an "economic cruising speed" of more than 2,500 words/minute and reaching heights of more than 4,000 words/minute. That's 70 words per second! He not only reads quickly, he also comprehends what he reads better than most people.

Today, Ramón is able to read, understand, and memorize faster than anyone in the world. He has also done stamina tests and holds world records for tasks such as the longest chain of words memorized in order, after hearing them only once and without seeing them: 23,200 words in 72 hours. He remembers the exact place of each word in the sequence. Due to his immense photographic memory, Ramón has also become specialized in memorizing only by hearing, not seeing, so as to "level the playing ground" for the rest of us mortals. In fact, he often works with his eyes blindfolded, and even then he is still able to memorize a Spanish deck of cards (40 cards) in only 40 seconds, without looking at them!

Stay tuned to Ramón's Websites (*www.ramoncampayo.com* and *www.speed-memory.com*) for more up-to-date information on his latest achievements and newest world records. Here are just a few of his most recent feats:

Memorization of six packs of cards (240), spread out on a table (blindfolded) after only hearing them once and in random order. Record memorization time of 18 exactly minutes. Recited all the cards without any mistakes.

Nine world records for fastest memorization obtained on November 7, 2004, in Starnberg (Germany), in five different trials. His current records are:

- 18-digit number in 0.5 seconds
- 19-digit number in 1 second

- 29-digit number in 4 seconds
- 100-digit number in 50 seconds
- 1,000-digit number in 15 minutes
- 34-digit binary number in 0,5 seconds
- 46-digit binary number in 1 second
- 56-digit binary number in 2 seconds
- 68-digit binary number in 3 seconds
- 80-digit binary number in 4 seconds

Ramón's reading speed is higher than 2,500 words per minute, more than 10 times the speed of an average university student.

He is a member of the International Society "MENSA," with 194 IQ points, one of the highest intellectual quotients in the world.

As an expert in study and memorization techniques, he prepares a multitude of students and public examiners, teaching them the secret intricacies of the mind during the learning and studying process. His students have obtained great results with his courses.

Ramón is the creator of "Speed-Memory" (*www.speed-memory.com*) which celebrates and coordinates international speed memory championships.

First place in the Open World Speed Memory Championship held April 28 to 29, 2007 in San Javier, Spain, and also first in the Open World Speed Memory Championship Munich 2009.

Ramón Campayo has broken more than 100 world records over the last five years, participating in around 40 international tournaments. He is currently the undefeated champion and holds all the world records in speed memory.